BURY ME
IN A
DIRTY
SUIT

**DISCOVERING MAN'S VALIANT PURPOSE
IN THE AFTERMATH OF 9/11**

DARIN KINDER

ENDORSEMENTS FOR *BURY ME IN A DIRTY SUIT*

"Using the backdrop of America's most tragic day, Darin inspires and equips men to courageously and actively pursue the will of God. His harrowing but humble account of his experience on 9/11 will leave you speechless. More importantly, Darin's teaching encourages men to step up, answer the call, and live with renewed purpose. With biblical teaching and even some humor, Darin provides the tools for the man of God to fight the good fight."

—WILLIAM G (JERRY) BOYKIN, LTG US Army (RET), Vice President, Family Research Council and former Delta Force Commander

"It's a privilege to read Kinder's words as he shares lessons from a life rich in struggle, scars, and success. Lessons applied on that day in September. There's not much room to learn on a day like that . . . only time to prove. He is a proven man. It's an honor to know him, and other heroes from that day and since. And humbling to watch him lead at the breakfast table the way he did on a battlefield on our own shores."

—CLINT BRUCE, Founder of TRG, Holdfast, & HighGroundHQ Foundation, Former Navy Seal

"*Bury Me in a Dirty Suit* reads like a modern-day battle cry. Darin Kinder doesn't just challenge men, he walks with us, shoulder to shoulder, calling us back to purpose, sacrifice, and Christlike strength. This book is raw, real, and rooted in gospel. It's not about polish—it's about presence. If you're ready to stop drifting and start fighting—for your faith, your family, and your brothers—this is your next step."

—DR. CHRIS HARPER, Chief Storyteller & CEO, BetterMan

"Every once in a while, you hear a story that stops you in your tracks—one that challenges you, wrecks you, and changes the way you see the world. That's what Darin Kinder's story of 9/11 has done for me since the first time I heard it over a decade ago. It's not just heroic and compelling—it's a wake-up call. In a world that leans hard into comfort and complacency, Darin reminds us that how we live our everyday moments matters deeply for the Kingdom. This book will stir something in you and leave you wanting a life with more purpose, more courage, and a journey that ends with a 'dirty suit.'"

—CYNTHIA YANOF, Podcaster, Speaker,
Author of *Life is Messy, God is Good*

"*Bury Me in a Dirty Suit* is a gritty, firsthand account of 9/11 told from the streets of Ground Zero. Darin Kinder doesn't just tell a story, he honors the fallen, celebrates the courage of first responders, and issues a bold call to action. With humility and conviction, he invites men to step into the purpose God has given them, not in theory, but in the thick of real life. This is a book that will challenge you, stir you, and equip you. By the end, Darin will have you convinced the best kind of suit is a dirty one."

—ADAM TARNOW, Co-author of *The Edge*
and Partner at PeopleWorks International

"Darin's story—his book, his life, his mission, and his legacy— isn't one of tragedy or suffering, but of triumph through faith. He is unique not just in his ability to express the lessons he learned during America's darkest day, but in his willingness to authentically share those lessons to help other men grow closer to each other and to God. I'm grateful for Darin's service, humility, friendship, and mentorship, and I'm confident others who read this book will gain much from it."

—DAN BRADLEY, Former USAF TACP,
President of The HighGroundHQ Foundation

"When I read *Bury Me in a Dirty Suit*, the following realities seemed to jump off the page at me: courageous, fierce, riveting, suspenseful, gut-wrenching, God-directed. I was captivated and changed—changed moment by moment as I was immersed into Darin's world and his story from 9/11. Then I felt compelled to reread it all over again. I felt all the same words and feelings, even deeper than the first reading. Now I want to give this book away, again and again. I've learned again with Darin: 'Jesus is enough'. He is always enough—more than enough."

—HAL HABECKER, Pastor,
Founder and President of Finishing Well Ministries

"Darin Kinder is a very rare individual—a man who understands exactly who he is and why God has placed him on this earth. *Bury Me in a Dirty Suit* is a captivating read that takes us along on Darin's compelling journey of self-discovery. But be warned . . . Darin's challenge to each of us is provocative and compelling. Don't read this unless you're ready, as Darin might put it, to get real with yourself and get your suit dirty!"

—RANKIN GASSAWAY, EVP & Chief
Administrative Officer, 7-Eleven, Inc. (retired)

422.

I dedicate this book to the 422 first responders who died in the line of duty responding to the terrorist attacks at the World Trade Center in New York City on September 11, 2001. These brave men and women willingly entered the fray. They chose to answer the bell! Each one was valiant until their last breath.

CONTENTS

Introduction   1

Chapter 1.   Get Into the Fight   7
Chapter 2.   How the Heck Did I End Up Here?   13
Chapter 3.   "Let's Go Be Heroes"   21
Chapter 4.   "So Others May Live"   29
Chapter 5.   Skyfall   37
Chapter 6.   Follow the Light   43
Chapter 7.   Be the Light   53
Chapter 8.   Tell Me Why   65
Chapter 9.   Citizens of a Republic   75
Chapter 10. Burning Ring of Fire   85
Chapter 11. Everything Has an Opposite   95
Chapter 12. Courage Is a Choice   109
Chapter 13. The Opposite of Fear Is Love   117
Chapter 14. Do the Next Thing   137
Chapter 15. Homecoming   147
Chapter 16. New Day, New Mission   155
Chapter 17. Time to Get Dirty   169
Chapter 18. No Safe Spaces   177
Chapter 19. His Will, Your Purpose   189
Chapter 20. What Is My Mission?   203
Chapter 21. Fight the Good Fight   215

Epilogue   227
Acknowledgments   231
About the Author   235

A coward dies a thousand times before his death,
but the valiant taste of death but once.

—William Shakespeare, *Julius Caesar*

INTRODUCTION

0959 HOURS, SEPTEMBER 11, 2001, WORLD TRADE CENTER, NEW YORK CITY

I'm dead. That was my first thought as I watched the top of World Trade Center (WTC) Tower 2 buckle, losing its battle with fire and gravity. I was simply too close. In my line of work, we call it "danger close." I was standing about halfway down the block on Church Street, less than a hundred yards from the base of Tower 2. Game over. Lights out. I'm done.

Run! That was my second thought. Later, I would come to understand it wasn't a thought at all. It wasn't an instinct or a result of training. It was a command from the Holy Spirit. Regardless, I much preferred the second thought, so I ran. I ran hard. Sprinting north half a block, with arms pumping and legs churning, I aggressively turned right onto Vesey Street. After all this time, it's still difficult to put into words the experience from ground level because everything moved so fast and the enormity of scale was overwhelming. Time was warped as I rode an emotional roller coaster, walking the thin line between courage and insanity.

Looking back, I wonder how I survived and why others didn't. I saw bodies with faces frozen in terror. I heard screams and sirens, oftentimes too similar to parse. These are the sights and sounds that still echo in my mind. As I ran, the dominant sound was the thunderclap of each floor collapsing upon the next, each collision bringing me closer to death and darkness.

The next sound at that moment reminds me of a freight train barreling down my back. I'm speaking of the massive storm cloud of debris. We have all seen the news footage of this man-made vortex. But very few experienced it. This is my story.

I was a fit twenty-seven-year-old Secret Service agent, so I ran pretty fast. But not fast enough. In mere seconds, that beautiful, clear, sunny September day became a dark night of horrors. Pitch black, I was immediately lost. I ran with my right arm extended outward while my left hand held the top of my shirt close around my mouth and nose. But my efforts were futile. My eyes, nose, and mouth were instantly filled with thick pulverized concrete and other particles. I coughed and spat as I ran, attempting to rid my mouth of the taste of industrial chalk. It tasted like chewing on a piece of drywall. The smell was like wet tar freshly applied to a highway.

Just as the storm overtook me, I was surrounded by large chunks of falling debris. As the darkness overcame me, debris was falling to my right and left, so I kept running. Today, I tell folks it sounded like cars falling from the sky, and that's not an exaggeration. Seconds later, I was clear of the falling debris, so I began to walk. I guess *stagger* would be more accurate. I could not see, and I could barely breathe. "Jesus, help me!" was all I could muster. It was enough. Jesus is always enough.

Why write a book about September 11 almost twenty-five years after the attack? Well, that's a complex question for me to tackle. And I'm looking forward to guiding you through the experience as I answer the question. But first, let me tell you where we are going. My desire is to walk you through my experience of that day, almost minute by minute. September 11, 2001, is a once-in-a-generation moment when *everyone* can recall exactly where they were and what they were doing. It is a shared experience on a national level. In a painful way, it ties us to each other. But there is so much more to my experience than just a recounting of actions or a sequence of events along a known timeline. In the midst of this intense and harrowing story, I want to share my evidence of God's faithfulness as He has made beauty from ashes in my life.

There's a famous old quote attributed to Samuel Clemens, better known as Mark Twain: "The two most important days in your life are the day you are born and the day you find out why." My experience has taught me a few things about purpose. A man without purpose, a higher calling, almost always becomes one of two things: a hyperambitious tyrant with an aggressive manner that leaves a path of destruction in his wake or the passive man with a defeatist mindset who is consistently ineffective in all his endeavors and never has an impact on the world. One is reckless; the other is feckless. In a way, both are destructive, and neither brings the light of Christ into a dark world.

The latter part of this book will address this larger issue of purpose in great detail. For now, I'll just say finding a higher purpose in life changes your world and the world around you. A properly placed purpose will allow those in your sphere of influence to flourish. You can become a small part of a bigger story and begin to serve something greater than yourself. My purpose is found in the eternal hope that is Jesus Christ. And that hope brings me, and it can bring you, joy and peace!

Each and every man and woman reading this book was created by God for a purpose. The Scriptures say we are each a unique masterpiece made for good works that He has prepared for us (Ephesians 2:10). We were made for this time and this place. Only God can give us a true mission and real meaning in life because we are merely the created and He is the Creator. I call that mission a valiant purpose. Why? Because we live in an upside-down world. We worship the created, not the Creator.

We are surrounded daily by the distractions and temptations of this life. We are bombarded with a single message: be happy and find that happiness only from within. Thus, living out God's will is challenging and uncomfortable. And in our modern mindsets, uncomfortable is often synonymous with unsafe. Therefore, seeking God's will and living out your God-ordained purpose will take courage. Real courage. Courage to live "against the grain" and courage to run headlong into the unknown. It will require a valiant heart. And that's just a glimpse of the joyful life driven by valiant purpose. I want to share mine and encourage you to seek yours.

When you finish this book, you will be challenged to change your life in ways that give you joy and bring glory to God. A courageous life of God-ordained mission and meaning awaits you. I will challenge you to boldly enter into His plan for your life so that you can have the humble honor of being used by God in His big story. It's gonna be intense, fierce, and even fun at times. Your journey to valiant purpose begins now. Buckle up!

PART I

BRING
THE LIGHT
TO THE FIGHT

CHAPTER 1

GET INTO THE FIGHT

Once more into the fray, into the last great fight I'll
ever know. To live and die on this day.
—*The Grey* (2011)

0846 HOURS, WORLD TRADE CENTER 7 (WTC 7), NINTH FLOOR

If this was another Navy SEAL book, I would tell you all about how I spent the morning working out on the shores of the Hudson River, getting wet and sandy while carrying a telephone pole along the beach. But no. In reality, after a grueling workout of weightlifting and running (on a treadmill, mind you, not *nearly* as exciting), I was getting cleaned up in the gym locker room of the United States Secret Service, or USSS, New York Field Office, donning dress clothes and shiny shoes and harboring a fair amount of good-natured attitude about it while New York's last moments of normalcy were slipping quietly away.

The only thing I hate more than a boring meeting, I thought, *is a boring meeting in a suit and tie.*

At the time, I was twenty-seven. I'd been an agent for less than two years, and I can assure you that at that age, I could have accurately been considered a young-and-dumb "baby agent," full stop. But in my defense, the suit and tie weren't a regular thing for agents at the New York Field Office, and it signaled the dull morning to come—one filled with briefings in preparation for the upcoming United Nations General Assembly to be held in the city later that month. But I digress. I schooled my attitude, threaded the tie under my collar, and lifted the two ends to knot it.

I never had the chance.

At 0846 hours, a faint vibration shuddered through the locker room. I felt it through the soles of my feet, heard it in the quiet rattle of furniture and—alarmingly—the building itself.

I couldn't have known at that moment that America had just been sucker punched. I couldn't have known that an unprecedented number of men and women in World Trade Center 1 and American Airlines Flight 11—innocent victims, dead on impact as their aircraft slammed into the north side of WTC 1—had just been killed. I couldn't have known they were joined in death by four radical Islamic extremists (cowards who will remain nameless here) who overtook the plane with unforgiving violence.

And yet they were gone, all the same.

The first volley in the battle of 9/11 had hit its mark with brutal precision.

It was the ultimate opening salvo in a surprise attack and, unfortunately, just the beginning. Within moments, our office personnel were instructed to evacuate the building immediately. Our office was located in WTC 7, the third tallest building of the World Trade Center complex. Most people don't even know that the World Trade Center complex consisted of seven buildings. Towers 1 and 2 obviously dominated

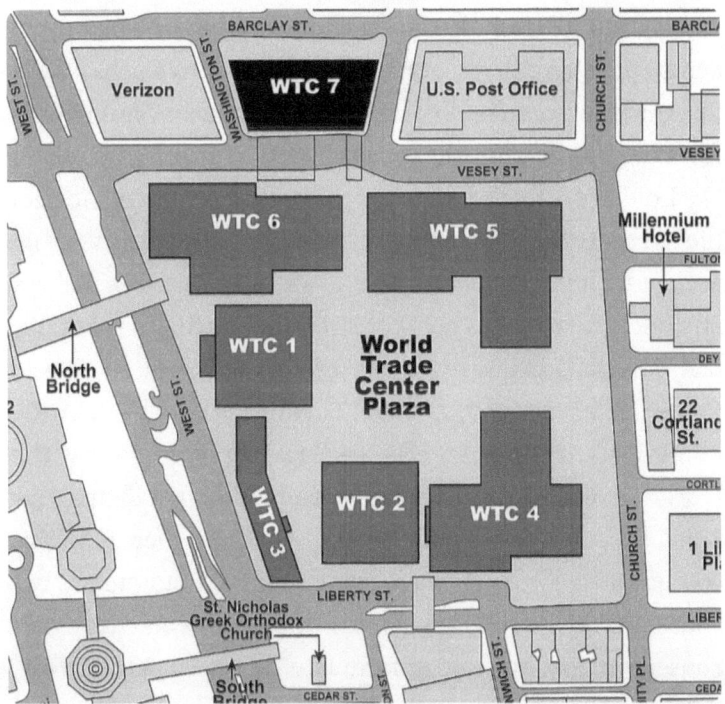

the landscape. In addition, the complex was bracketed by four shorter buildings on each corner of the complex, WTC 3, 4, 5, and 6. WTC 7 was the newest structure of the World Trade Center, and it was located directly across the street (north) from WTC 1 (see map above).

I stood in the gym and took a moment to collect my thoughts. I didn't know exactly what was going on, but I decided to climb one flight of stairs to grab some gear from my desk. I hastily put on my gun, badge, spare magazine, and handcuffs, not realizing I would use none of them that day. In my haste, I neglected to grab the three items I would desperately need later: my handheld radio, everyday-carry knife, and flashlight. Like I said, I was young and dumb. I found a small group of agents gathered around a window, looking out across the street to the north side of WTC 1. What I saw will forever be emblazoned in my mind. Smoke and fire poured from the tower, and light debris floated to the ground.

I did not know what had happened, and I had no idea of the enormity of the situation, but I knew one thing: this was no accident! I immediately assumed it was a terror attack. Being a student of history and my USSS training convinced me of this fact. After all, this wasn't the first terror attack on the World Trade Center. In 1993, a radical Islamic terror cell led by the blind Sheik Rahman and Ramzi Yousef tried to destroy the World Trade Center with a truck bomb. Although their attack killed six and injured more than a thousand, their objective was not met. They may have failed in their first attempt, but Yousef would later pledge that his "brothers" would try again. Yousef was pure evil, and unfortunately, he was correct. While watching WTC 1 burn, I recall my immediate thoughts. I'm not proud of them, nor am I ashamed. Being a Christian, you might think my first thoughts were a prayer for the victims, compassion for those trapped, or just plain stunned denial. Nope! I was pissed off and looking to fight.

As I watched the top of WTC 1 burn, *Get into the fight* went through my mind. It's a concept that was drilled into my head as a boy by my father. I apply those words to every aspect of my life. My father lived a hard life, and he battled his fair share of demons. He did not teach me much in regard to faith. But he was a fighter. He was fierce! And he raised his sons to get into the fight. In the Christian walk, there are times for prayer, compassion, and condolences. But there are also times to enter into the fray, get bloody, get dirty, and fight evil. This was time for the latter. But let's be perfectly clear. Sometimes, even most times, "fighting evil" takes the form of selfless sacrifice, service, and acts of compassion. Simply bringing light into darkness. I entered into the fight, but I didn't need my weapons or handcuffs. I just needed the love of Christ to cast out my fears.

We proceeded to evacuate from the main lobby onto Vesey Street, which was directly across from WTC 1. A large number of USSS personnel had gathered and were wondering how we should proceed. A group of agents had the thoughtful idea that we could assist in the emergency response by utilizing our first aid trauma (FAT) kits. The USSS FAT kit is a large backpack-sized kit filled with an ungodly amount of first aid and trauma gear for a number of different medical emergencies. Needless to say, a FAT kit is heavy and almost always carried by the junior agent on every detail. So, a group of agents dashed up three flights of stairs to our office in WTC 7 and returned soon after with a number of FAT kits. In the meantime, we learned a large group of Fire Department of New York (FDNY) ambulances had marshaled on the West Side Highway and were beginning to render medical care to wounded victims. As a group, we made a decision: that's where we would enter the fray, get dirty, and get into the fight.

As we jogged to West Street, my friend and colleague Wayne said something to me. I can't remember his exact words, but it was something like "What do you think we do now?" I certainly remember my short response, word for word. I have shared this story and testimony with thousands over the years, yet I have never shared this publicly. That's because my response has troubled me for quite some time.

Because it sounds like a brash and arrogant declaration from a naive glory hound. But now, over twenty years later, I am comfortable with my response. Because I know it sprung from a valiant heart rooted in fierce faith. I know that God now uses this fierceness for His purpose as I play a small role in His big story. Now, as a father of four sons, my prayer is that the same fierce faith will come to pour from their hearts as well. So, what was my response?

"Let's go be heroes."

CHAPTER 2

HOW THE HECK DID I END UP HERE?

*For I know the plans I have for you, declares the Lord,
plans for welfare and not for evil, to give you a future
and a hope.*
—Jeremiah 29:11

If you knew me, you would be asking the same question. I was a Secret Service agent for over twenty-five years. I lived and witnessed history and traveled to forty countries around the globe. I protected presidents, vice presidents, former presidents, and countless foreign heads of state. There were many sacrifices along the way, but I feel very blessed to have served my nation in a noble pursuit. Yet still, there were many times in my career when I would pose the question to myself: *How did I get here?*

The big answer is that God's will is my purpose, even when I had no idea what was going on. Much more on that later. But specifically on 9/11, I remember literally asking myself this question as we jogged to the first aid trauma station on the West Side Highway. So, let's get to know each other a bit.

Service: A Family Tradition

I grew up in the small town of Mechanicsville, located in central Virginia. My brother (the real cop in the family) and I shared in a bit of an identity crisis. That's because my mother was from a farm in central Ohio, and my father hailed from a working-class family in the hills of East Tennessee. In general terms, the Ohio side of the family was sincere, hardworking, well-educated, soft-spoken Quakers, with a steady, quiet faith that undergirded their lives; the Tennessee clan was hardworking, loud, and possessed blue-collar feistiness with Baptist roots that ran a mile deep. To complicate matters, my mother and father raised their sons in central Virginia. When we visited Ohio, we were the rednecks from the South. But our Tennessee clan viewed us Yankees from the North. Like I said, an identity crisis. Because of this, I never quite planted roots in Virginia. My eyes were always on the horizon, looking for a place to land and make my own mark. I believe that's exactly how I landed in the Secret Service and working in New York City.

We grew up in a loving environment and lived an idyllic young life. My father worked for a state agency serving the blind, and my mother was a registered nurse. You could say that "service" was kind of baked into our souls. My older brother, Doug, seemed to be drawn to law enforcement at an early age. Meanwhile, I was fixated on serving in the United States military. Being children of the '80s, we were "raised on Reagan" and moved through life with confidence and aggressiveness. The America I grew up in was bold, confident, and embraced a full-throated belief in American exceptionalism. We were brothers, only three years apart, so we fought like crazy. Naturally. But my brother has a kind soul, and he never physically destroyed me, although he could have—many times. He saved his mean streak for any older kid that messed with his little brother. And with me being a sarcastic young punk, his services were called upon more than once. We may have fought each other, but we saved most of our fierceness for fighting for each other. We were brothers. He would later graduate from college and enter into a long career of noble service with the sheriff's department in our hometown.

I, on the other hand, planned to enter the US military upon completion of college. It was just a decision between the US Navy and the United States Marine Corps, or so I thought. Have I mentioned I was young and dumb? Just to prove it to you, in my last semester of college, I began the process of entering the military. It didn't last long. I was stunned to learn that I was medically disqualified from service because of my history of asthma. I had struggled with it as a child, and remnants of the respiratory ailment lasted into my college years. I was shocked, baffled, and disappointed. And for the first time in my life, I felt purposeless.

Fortunately for me, I didn't feel purposeless for long. I had always dreamed of serving in the US military, but I had a fallback plan. So, I fell back. I graduated from James Madison University in 1996 with a degree in interdisciplinary social studies and education. So, I became a high school history teacher. And I loved it. I got a job teaching world history to ninth graders at Clover Hill High School in Chesterfield County, Virginia, just two counties to the south of Mechanicsville. Sandwiched between the two counties was the city of Richmond. Growing up in Mechanicsville, I thought the "south side" of Richmond was the other side of the world. Little did I know my future Secret Service career would take me to forty countries around the globe.

Regardless, I poured myself into my new job and quickly realized I was pretty good at telling stories and connecting with young people. Properly planning lessons and administrative duties, well, we all have our weaknesses. I coached ninth grade and junior varsity basketball as well, loving every minute of it. To top it all off, I began dating one of my good friends from college, Heather. Life was good. Life was fun. Life was safe. But deep down, I had always felt I wasn't created to feel safe. It spawned an itch in me that still needed to be scratched.

It appears God was ready to give me a nudge from my "safe" zone. My good friend Billy taught school with me in the social studies department. Billy had a neighbor named Brandon, who happened to be a Secret Service agent in the Richmond Field Office. Sometime in early 1997, at the request of Billy, Brandon was at our high school one day speaking to Billy's US government classes. I'll never forget that day. I was at my desk in the social studies department room during my planning period, creating a masterful lesson plan. (Probably not.) Billy introduced me to Brandon, and he agreed to chat about his career.

At that point, I had never considered a career in federal law enforcement, especially the Secret Service. But there was something impressive about Brandon. He was huge but humble. He was serious but affable. He was fierce but steady. He was a lion, strength under control. So, I sat down with Brandon and asked him no less than two hundred questions about the Secret Service. He was patient with me and very informative. He knew I was interested and gave me his business card. I remember being impressed by him and flattered that he thought maybe I had what it takes to be a Secret Service agent.

That night, I placed the business card in my bedside drawer. My brother was already well into his law enforcement career, so this was not a foreign idea to me. I didn't know the path of my journey forward. But I knew I wanted to serve my country in some manner. I thought about it, prayed about it, and sought the counsel of wise individuals. Yet the business card remained in the bedside drawer. I taught and coached another year and became engaged, with the card still in the bedside drawer. I entered year three of my teaching career with much contentment and success. And by the way, I got married in 1998! The card, however, was still in the bedside drawer.

The young woman who rocked my world was Heather Inkman. I met Heather at college the first weekend of my junior year. She was a spitfire. She had a contagious energy and a laugh that would turn the heads in a room. I would come to realize that she was driven, disciplined, principled, and a bold follower of Jesus. She would go on to help nurture those same traits in me. Simply put, she was a blessing dropped into my life that I did not deserve. We were great friends for two years as we traversed the mistakes and successes of our college years. I graduated in 1996, and she still had one year remaining in her pursuit of a nursing degree. Since I was young and dumb (a theme), we never dated while we were in school. We began seeing each other during my first year of teaching only because our friends made it happen. By the time she was set to graduate, we were a serious thing.

She was bold and adventurous. She had plans to enter the United States Air Force as an officer and serve as a nurse. We were at a crossroads. At this point in our relationship, I saw in her the character trait that best defines her spirit. Selflessness. She put her plans on hold, moved to Richmond, and got a job as a nurse in an inner-city hospital. I knew the ball was in my court. I wasn't that young and dumb. In late 1997, I asked her to be my bride, and we were married in 1998. But here's the thing. She still had bold adventure in her bones. I still had a heart of service and a nagging itch that needed to be scratched. We were made for this. We talked about it, prayed about it, and kept putting off a decision. I was restless and uneasy. That "itch" kept getting more pronounced. I loved teaching, but I knew, in my innermost core, I was not living out God's will for my life. I had to answer the call, and by God's sovereign grace, he had coupled me with the perfect wife for such a bold change of course. God comes first in my life, and my purpose is to faithfully follow His will. Therefore, safety is a third priority. So, I opened that bedside drawer, picked up the card, and dialed the number.

The Adventure Begins

The next twelve months were a blur. I entered into the Secret Service hiring process in just the right season. At that time, a significant portion of the agent population was eligible or near eligible to retire. They were putting on a full-court press in their hiring initiative. The Secret Service typically prefers prior military or law enforcement experience. I brought neither to the table. But God's timing is perfect, and I guess I was just well-rounded enough to make the cut. I was hired as a Special Agent in the New York Field Office on February 28, 2000.

Funny story: Several years later, in New York City, I was working another United Nations General Assembly (UNGA) assignment when I bumped into Ray, a veteran agent from the Richmond Field Office. A few years earlier, Ray had been one of the senior agents on my hiring panel, and he had thoroughly enjoyed busting my balls with questions and scenarios to determine whether I would make the cut. We sat down for lunch, and I thanked Ray for his role in bringing me on board the Secret Service. Without missing a beat and between bites of his sandwich, Ray deadpanned, "Yeah, you didn't really check all the boxes we were looking for, but we liked you." Funny. I took it as an insult wrapped in a compliment and just laughed.

After being hired, I completed seven months of intensive training and was convinced I was ready to tackle the world. Or so I thought. I reported to the New York Field Office, located in 7 World Trade Center in August of 2000. I'll never forget laying eyes on the World Trade Center that first August morning. I had taken the NY/NJ PATH train from our apartment in Hoboken, New Jersey. I walked up and out of the underground platform and stood motionless. Stunned. Small-town kid in the big city. I was slightly nervous and intimidated, but I moved like a young man with purpose, ready to make a mark. Young and dumb but wanting to be unleashed, Heather and I began our life in New York City.

CHAPTER 3

"LET'S GO BE HEROES"

Courage is being scared to death and saddling up anyway.
—John Wayne

0903 HOURS, SEPTEMBER 11, 2001, WORLD TRADE CENTER, WEST STREET, NEW YORK CITY

"Let's go be heroes." In that spirit, our large group of Secret Service agents arrived at the makeshift first aid area on the West Side Highway with our FAT kits in tow. I immediately began tending to a woman's arm. It was badly burned, and to be honest, my mind went blank. Luckily, an FDNY Paramedic was over my shoulder, tending to another victim. He yelled instructions at me step by step as I irrigated and bandaged her arm. When I say "yelled," I mean literally. This guy was classic FDNY, stereotypical New York City attitude. He may have been shouting proper instructions, but his tone said, "Hey moron, you're doing it all wrong!" Yep, even in crisis, the NYC spirit lives on.

Anyway, I never finished wrapping her arm. My focus was shattered by a massive explosion directly over my head. I didn't know it yet, but United Airlines Flight 175 had just slammed into WTC 2, the South Tower. If you remember, the second plane came in significantly lower than the first.

To make matters worse, I was a hundred yards or less from the base of the tower. Oddly enough, I never heard or saw the plane because I had tunnel vision on my task, wrapping the woman's arm. But immediately, I was snapped back into reality.

The world was falling all around me as debris from the plane, chunks of the building, and burning jet fuel rained down. We were in the kill zone. It has been well documented that several victims trapped in the towers made the conscious decision to leap from the building rather than burn to death. The choice is unimaginable for those watching. Fortunately, the Lord spared me from seeing any "jumpers" on September 11, 2001. Apparently, several fell in my immediate area, as witnessed by several of my coworkers. In regard to the woman I was tending to, I'm not sure what happened to her because we all scattered like ants in the chaos.

I never saw her again. I was too busy running for cover.

I landed under a metal portico on the sidewalk with two other Secret Service agents, Tom Armas and John Buckley. As we tried to assess the situation, none of us fully realized the magnitude of the attack. Although the destruction was obvious, I did not know two 767s had served as missiles in this attack. I confess to you today that, had I known all the facts at the time, I probably would not have entered the fray. Tom was the first to speak. Being a Marine and a fine leader, he suggested we enter the lobby of the WTC to assist in the evacuation. Now, you should know. Listening to and following a jarhead will sometimes get you in trouble and maybe even killed. But it was the right call to make. So, we scampered across the street, dodging debris as we ran. It was time to answer the bell.

Answer the Bell—It's Your Calling

Answer the bell. I've used that term once already. Allow me to explain. I love the sweet science of boxing. Many of the "heroes" of my youth were boxing greats—Muhammad Ali, Ray Leonard, and *any* young prodigy who wore USA on their jerseys in the Olympics. And, of course, Rocky! Anyway, two fighters square off, wait in their corners, and listen for the bell. When the bell rings, they make a choice. They fight, or they take the path of least resistance. In the fight, they get beaten and bloodied, but they also land their own shots. They experience victory and defeat. They feel the joy and the pain, often in the same round. Teddy Roosevelt once famously said that men like this choose to fight in the arena "so that his place shall never be with those cold and timid souls who neither know victory nor defeat." On the other hand, there is an easier route. The fighter who doesn't answer the bell stays in his corner where it is "safe" or walks away when it gets too hard. He quits.

Roberto Duran was a Panamanian boxer who fought professionally for over thirty years, from 1968 to 2001. Duran was a brawler whose punching power earned him the nickname Hands of Stone. Roberto Duran was a great fighter! He was a four-time world champion over four different weight classes and is often listed in some publications as one of the top twenty fighters of all time. He fought in the golden era of lightweight and welterweight boxing of the 1970s and '80s. Duran valiantly competed against boxing legends such as "Marvelous" Marvin Hagler and Thomas "The Hit Man" Hearns. However, Duran is best known for his thrilling trilogy of bouts with "Sugar" Ray Leonard. Leonard was an American hero with a huge following after he won the gold medal in the 1976 Olympic Games. He was on top of the boxing world until he ran into the Hands of Stone. On June 20, 1980, Duran and Leonard went toe-to-toe in what became known as "The Brawl in Montreal." Duran won the grueling fifteen-round fight by unanimous decision, capturing the WBC Welterweight world title. Duran was now a world champion for the second time. See, I told you. Roberto Duran was a great fighter.

However, that is not how Duran is remembered by most. He is remembered for supposedly uttering two words, "No más," which translates to "No more." Here's the story. Duran and Leonard met five months later in a rematch held in New Orleans. It was billed as "The Super Fight," possibly the most anticipated rematch in boxing history at the time. This fight would end very differently. After six rounds, the fight was extremely close on the scorecards. In the seventh round, Leonard deployed a new tactic. He began taunting Duran in various ways, using his superior speed to avoid Duran's angry and wild punches. The humiliation reached its climax at the end of the round when Leonard mockingly wound up his right hand for a silly "bolo" punch and then smashed a left jab into Duran's face.

The wheels came off for Duran in the eighth round. He had been embarrassed and was fighting angry and reckless. He continuously moved forward in a wild manner, trying to unleash on Leonard. But "Sugar" Ray was too fast, too smart. Now, his speed and precision were making Duran pay for his undisciplined approach. Leonard was putting an old-school beatdown on Duran. And then it happened. With thirty seconds remaining in the round, Duran turned his back to

Leonard and quit. As the referee tried to call them both back to the middle of the ring, Duran waved his hand at him and repeatedly said, "No más." The fight was over. Leonard was the champ. Duran was the chump.

Roberto Duran was a great fighter, a four-time world champion. But even today, he is mostly remembered as the guy who quit. He didn't answer the bell. That is his legacy. To be fair, Duran has always denied uttering the words "No más" and has given several reasons for walking away. But he cannot deny the obvious. He quit.

Men, we need to battle. We need to enter the fray. We need to answer the bell. If we stay in our "safe place," we may avoid getting knocked out, but we will never win glory. We will never experience the pain of metaphorically taking a right cross to the jaw or the agony of a body blow to the kidney. But we also will never feel the joy of buckling the Enemy's knees after landing our own left hook. If you are reading this and you are a Christian, let me be very clear. Our God calls us to answer the bell so that our works will win glory. But not our glory, God's glory.

When we battle evil, when we enter into other's pain and suffering, when we fight to push back darkness, then we are seizing a God-ordained opportunity to serve Him. So that His glory might be known. Safety and comfort are often not part of His plan. Men, hear me clearly! Safe is boring. Safe is comfortable. Safe is lazy. Safe doesn't strike fear in the heart of the Enemy. God does not call us to live "the safe life." God's will is your purpose, and your safety is a distant third priority. He built you for a reason, for a purpose, for a fight. Discerning that purpose and choosing to courageously pursue it is the next step in your spiritual journey. It's the heart and soul of this book. We will completely unpack this concept in part IV.

This World Needs Heroes

This chapter began with the bold declaration: "Let's go be heroes." In the spirit of Austin Powers, "Allow myself to explain . . . myself." What is a hero? Well, Dictionary.com defines it as "a person noted for courageous acts or nobility of character." I would take it a few steps further. I would say it's a man or woman who faces a known danger and is willing to serve and sacrifice for the sake of others in the face of fear beyond what they can endure. Only to find they possess the grit and mettle to persevere beyond their known limits. We can debate what makes a hero, but one thing is for certain: a hero, I am not. When someone hears my story and calls me a hero, it makes me extremely uncomfortable.

I was awarded the US Secret Service Medal of Valor for my actions on September 11, 2001, but that doesn't make me special. I do not consider myself a hero at all. Not even close. While my actions can be considered service and came at the sacrifice of my well-being, I do not match my own definition of a hero. Because for most of the day, I did not have an accurate and comprehensive awareness of the situation. Like I said before, I never realized two 767 jet airliners had slammed into the World Trade Center.

Honestly, if I had all the facts on the ground, then my actions may have been different. So, let me be very clear. The heroes of that day in New York City were the 422 first responders who perished and the many more who entered the fray at Ground Zero and lived to fight another day. These brave men and women had all the facts, knew the danger, and knew the cost. Yet they chose to run to the threat; they answered the bell. Courage is a choice. While most people ran from the danger, they looked past it and got into the fight. Men and women who lived with a valiant purpose to serve others and pay whatever price was necessary. May they forever be honored and may they never be forgotten.

In regard to "Let's go be heroes," that deserves an explanation. Those words came from a simple guy who didn't have any of the answers. But I was going to choose to help in any way I could. I was making a choice not to follow the crowd and not to be ordinary. I was not moving forward to save lives and make the newspapers! I was just willing to put my ass on the line to help others. It was the right thing to do. I was simply moving forward to do the next thing, then the next thing, and then the next thing. Young, dumb, and terribly afraid, I was choosing to enter into people's hurt and bring a little light into their darkness. That's it. That's what I meant when I said those words. I think a hero is more about the heart and less about the outcome.

But there is something more we can draw from this experience. There's another point I want to make that I think all of us can apply to our lives. Here it is. I simply chose, on repeat, to do the next thing. Sometimes that's the best we can do. Courage is a choice followed by action, not some high-minded idea. I did not have a grand plan for the day. I did not have a big goal to accomplish or a massive problem to solve. I didn't have all the answers because I didn't even have all the facts. In a way, I was lost. But I was lost and with a purpose.

At the time, I had no way of knowing what the totality of my contributions would be at the end of the day. I had no clue about the final outcome. So, I had a choice to make. Call it a lost cause and run? Or serve and fight in some little way by just doing the next thing. There it is, as simple as can be. Sometimes, we just have to do the next thing.

A dear friend of mine, Cynthia Yanof, is fond of saying, "Life is messy. God is good." Both are true indeed. Life can quickly get dark and dirty. But God made us for this time and this place. And He created each one of us with unique skills and abilities. There are huge problems in this world that can seem impossible to solve. Quick question: How does a lion eat an elephant? One bite at a time. That's what I call just doing the next thing. It does not require a five-year plan, the formation of a committee, or a nonprofit organization. Sometimes, we just have to handle the next small problem before us. Just do the next thing on repeat. As you will see, this mindset builds on itself throughout my entire experience on September 11. By the end of the day, I had a remarkable story to share with the perfect blend of bravery and foolishness. But the remarkable story was built step by step, just doing the next thing in front of me. Helping the next person, climbing the next set of stairs, or fighting the next fire. Just doing the next thing. I think we can all take that lesson and apply it to our lives. Will you?

CHAPTER 4

"SO OTHERS MAY LIVE"

Greater love has no one than this, that someone lay down his life for his friends.
—John 15:13

0907 HOURS, SEPTEMBER 11, 2001, WORLD TRADE CENTER, WEST STREET, NEW YORK CITY.

Tom, John, and I entered WTC 1 (North Tower) through a door at the ground level. In my mind today, the scene is a puzzling contradiction. There were alarms blaring, but it was somehow eerily quiet. In a sense, the noise was all alarms but nothing else. To make matters even stranger, in many places, there was about an inch of water covering the floors. My assumption is the fire sprinklers had run for quite some time but they were now off in the lobby. The three of us sloshed through the water as we slow-jogged around the massive lobby, looking for people to help. Eventually, we found a stairwell with a steady stream of people evacuating down.

Time to Do the Next Thing

We entered the stairwell and noticed the evacuation was orderly and fairly tame. Not knowing what the immediate future held, we simply began to slow jog up the steps. One step at a time, we climbed, looking for people who needed assistance. It didn't take us long. As we reached somewhere around the tenth floor, we encountered a woman in desperate need. She was very large, overweight, exhausted, and slumped over in the corner of the stairwell. She was clearly no longer able to evacuate herself. Seeing her condition completely stopped me in my tracks. She gave every indication that she was broken and defeated. But to my consternation, dozens of able-bodied men were passing her by as they evacuated down the stairs. It was stunning. I don't think it was selfishness or a lack of human decency. I just think they had tunnel vision. They had a laser focus on getting out. Focused on the next stair step in front of them instead of the next human. Focused on their fear, not love.

Before we go on judging these people, we should take a moment to consider our own daily walk in life. How many of us are hyperfocused on the busyness of our lives? Me, for one. I'm talking about the kid's school, youth sports events, work-related problems and successes, the messy marriage, the lover you adore, the promotion you eye. Maybe your focus is social media likes, the perfect storyboard on Instagram, or just the endless quest to be the perfect parent/spouse. We can all get tunnel vision on something. And that means we miss the things hiding in plain sight. We miss the hurt in our communities all around us. We miss the broken marriage next door. We miss the exploitation of children right under our noses. We miss the child sex trafficking across the street on a Saturday night while we hang out with friends in the cool part of town. We miss abuse. We miss the starving and the homeless. Because we have tunnel vision in our own lives, maybe even on our own survival. Do any of you fall into these categories? I'm raising my hand right now. It's time we wake up and see the darkness closing in all around us.

The men and women in the unknown stairwell of World Trade Center 1 were no different—they just needed to be awakened to the situation happening in front of them. I told Tom and John that I would carry the exhausted woman down to safety, and we agreed to meet up at the next point of need in the stairwell.

It would be the last time I saw Tom and John that day.

I helped the woman to her feet and began to carry her down—but at five feet, ten inches, and 175 pounds, I was going nowhere. I lasted two steps before accepting that it was a two-man job. So, I grabbed a random dude—literally by the collar—and snapped him out of his tunnel vision as I instructed him to give me a hand. He quickly agreed.

Together, we carefully navigated the woman down the ten or so flights of stairs. Luckily, a pair of FDNY paramedics had stationed themselves at the bottom of the stairwell to receive any injured civilians. We handed her off to the paramedics, shook hands, and parted company as I returned to the stairwell.

And thus began a period of great uneasiness for me.

Up until that moment, I had been serving shoulder to shoulder with other USSS agents. We were making a difference, and we were doing it as a team. But for the first time that day, I was alone. I was separated from my colleagues—my guys—and I wasn't fond of the feeling. Moving forward that day, most of my motivation in what I did was to reconnect with them.

Although I spent twenty-five years working with the finest men and women this country has to offer and can say without hesitation that female agents are a tremendous asset to the US Secret Service, it just so happened that on 9/11, all of my service was with other men in my agency. So, when I refer to my colleagues as "my guys," that's why. I had only been working with other men that day, and in the pressure cooker of those events, I experienced a driving force to join up with my guys.

So, I went looking for them.

Let's take a break here to address another aspect of the Christian life. We, as men and women, are designed by God to live in community. Life is better and our "works" are more effective when done in community with other believers. When we engage in the Lord's work together, we harness all of our God-given talents, strengths, and abilities to bring the full force of God's grace into the broken places. In the military and law enforcement circles, we call that a force multiplier. Christian men, especially, are more effective when working in community and our faith is strengthened when we serve shoulder to shoulder. We can hold each other accountable, lift each other up when weak, and experience greater joy in the fight! Isolation is not the answer. "Lone-wolf" Christians typically burn out in frustration or, even worse, fall into unrepentant sin. I encourage you, as you process the challenges proposed in this book, to link up with other like-minded godly men as you tackle the Christian life. Find your "guys." Find your "people." And then get busy discovering your valiant purpose and answer the bell of God's call on your hearts to have an impact for Christ.

Next, I reentered the stairwell with two objectives: help others in need and find "my guys." I climbed and climbed, passing evacuating people along the way. Time to make another "young-and-dumb" revelation about myself. I remember climbing flight after flight. And as I went, I was attempting to say encouraging words to the civilians as we passed in opposite directions. I don't remember everything I said, but I do remember uttering this haunting phrase several times: "Don't worry. Nothing can bring these towers down." Ugh. Courage is a good attribute. But if I was making a recipe for courage, the list of ingredients would definitely include naïveté and ignorance. I guess "young and dumb" has its benefits.

Eventually, I climbed as high as about the thirtieth floor. For reference, each WTC tower was 110 floors. I stopped there because the door to the interior hallway was propped open. As I entered the hallway I encountered a scene forever emblazoned in my mind. I looked to my right to see the entire hallway lined with New York City firefighters. They were beaten, scarred, bloodied, and covered in soot. I'm not certain, but it looked as if they had been pulled back to regroup, refit, and reassess. I asked a couple of them if they had seen two Secret Service guys running around, Tom and John. To my surprise, they answered in the affirmative! I was shocked. Yes, I was gonna regroup with "my guys"! Unfortunately, the firefighters hadn't seen them in a while and were not able to even point me in the right direction. I was disappointed and had reached a decision point.

What should I do? Continue to climb in hopes of finding Tom and John? Or return down the stairwell to maybe regroup with other colleagues outside?

I took a deep breath and ran the odds through my head. Tom and John could be anywhere in the building, and I had no way to communicate with them. I had no comms as I had left my pager (remember those?) and cell phone in the gym locker and my handheld radio at my desk. Young and dumb. I made the decision to head back down. I thanked the firefighters and pivoted to the stairwell. And then it happened. I heard a loud command given by the FDNY commander in the hallway. His words will echo in my mind for eternity. Those words now serve as the source of my tremendous respect and admiration for the firefighting community. Those words haunted me for years. His words? "Get your gear together, boys. We're going back up."

Need heroes? Look no further.

As long as this nation still produces men and women like this, then I still have hope. They knew the danger, and they were fully aware of the price to be paid. And they went up anyway! Their devotion to the mission and each other still brings me to tears. I have no way of knowing for sure, but I can only assume that the men in that hallway are members of the 343. That's the 343 FDNY firefighters killed on September 11, 2001. They went back up the tower to save the lives of others.

It reminds me of another group of brave men and women I have worked with during my career. In my time with the Secret Service, I was honored to serve my agency in my capacity as a USSS Rescue Swimmer. During that time, I had the distinct privilege of training with the elite Rescue Swimmers from the United States Coast Guard. I have always been fond of their motto: "So others may live." That motto comes to mind when I remember the fallen first responders of 9/11. The 343 certainly embodied the "So others may live" motto. Their deaths were not in vain. Not only did they save lives that day, but their valiant sacrifice serves as inspiration and motivation for countless young firefighters today. Young people who not only remember the fallen but serve their communities every day to honor the fallen. I thank God for them all!

CHAPTER 5

SKYFALL

*The heart of a man plans his way but the Lord
establishes his steps.*
—Proverbs 16:9

0933 HOURS, SEPTEMBER 11, 2001, APPROXIMATELY 30TH FLOOR, WTC 1, NEW YORK CITY

I once again entered the stairwell to head back down to ground level. I had decided to try to rendezvous with other USSS colleagues outside. By this time, the traffic in the stairwell was almost nonexistent. My guess is most people had been able to evacuate already, or they were tragically trapped above the impact zone, unable to use the stairwell. Along the way, I encountered a similar situation as before. There was an overweight woman who was exhausted, unable to traverse any more flights. I helped her get to her feet, and I guided her down. She was able to do most of the work under her own power, so I didn't need to carry her much. Again, I handed her off to some paramedics at the base of the stairwell. Then I began to search for an exit to the central outdoor plaza of the WTC complex. Time to link up with my guys!

While I desired deeply to join forces with my colleagues, there was another need that had to be addressed first. I was thinking of the love of my life. While passing the lobby of WTC 1, I had a brilliant idea. And by brilliant, I sarcastically mean a really stupid idea. I noticed many FDNY fire commanders were manning the desk phones in the lobby. So, I said to myself, *Self, now would be a great time to call your wife.* I know. I know. You're screaming, "Get out of the building!" Did I mention young and dumb yet? Since the desk phones were being used, I approached a pay phone to call my wife.

As luck would have it, I didn't have any coins, but I grabbed the tethered phone anyway and punched in the number to make a collect call. The phone seemed to ring for an eternity, and then she answered. Heather was concerned but calm (as always), and a very brief conversation followed. I told her I was uninjured and in the WTC helping others evacuate. I was focused and in a bit of a zone. If you know Heather, then you would not be surprised to hear she was calm and steady on the phone. The woman was and has always been a rock. I am the "softie" in the relationship. She expressed her relief that I was OK, and we quickly said, "I love you," to each other and hung up. I immediately walked out the door and headed east across the plaza, stopping at about the midpoint of the complex on Church Street. But at this point, my story with Heather takes a turn for the worse.

This is where her nightmare begins. And it was my fault.

Heather did not know I had left the building immediately after our call. She did know, however, that exactly thirteen minutes later, WTC 2 collapsed. I know it was thirteen minutes because we later received the bill from the collect call. In thirteen minutes, she went from relief to despair. Heather watched her husband die on live TV, in living color. At least, that's what she thought. She had every reason to believe I was still in the building. To make matters worse, in those thirteen minutes, she had called my parents, my brother, her parents, her brother, and some friends. She did the right thing. They had been contacting her all morning, starving for information about my well-being. She told them all I had called, where I was, and what I was doing. She told them I was safe. Now they, too, tragically watched me die on live TV. If I could change any of my actions on 9/11, it would be never picking up the phone. I put Heather and our families through hours of gut-wrenching pain. It still brings me to tears today.

At that moment, everyone important in my life thought I was dead. Well, I wasn't dead, but I was just about to start fighting for my life. I walked to the far eastern perimeter of the WTC complex with one single objective in mind. Link up with my guys. I was walking and searching with purpose but to no avail. I didn't like the feeling of loneliness and isolation. It's a challenging feeling to explain. My experience that day was filled with chaos and fear, but whenever I was standing shoulder to shoulder with my brothers, there was a sense of calm and cool confidence. That's how we do the job. Whether it's Secret Service, police, firefighters, or military members, standing shoulder to shoulder with mission-minded brothers (and sisters) is the best part of the job. But at this moment, I was alone. I was standing halfway down the block on Church Street, and I began a conversation with a female NYPD officer. I was asking her if she had seen any Secret Service agents in the area. Then it happened. I began to hear a strange, high-pitched metal-on-metal screeching sound. Skyfall.

0959 HOURS, WORLD TRADE CENTER, CHURCH STREET, NEW YORK CITY

The South Tower (WTC 2) was collapsing. As I mentioned earlier, when WTC 2 buckled, I was approximately a hundred yards from its base. Way too close. And I'm embarrassed to say I almost immediately quit. *I'm dead. Game over*, I thought.

But God chose to kick me in the tail, forcing me to get back in the fight. Sometimes, that means simply surviving to fight another day. To die another day. And sometimes, that just means doing the next thing. The "next thing" for me was running like hell. So, I sprinted north up Church Street and immediately came to another decision point. As I ran up the block, I noticed an FDNY fire truck. For a moment, I considered sliding under the fire truck for cover because I knew the sky was literally falling upon me. I pictured myself sliding under the truck like a baseball player sliding into home plate. I even took a step in the direction of the truck, but for some reason, I bypassed the truck and continued sprinting up the block.

My legs pumped as I turned hard right onto Vesey Street. The thunderclaps were getting louder, each floor pancaking into the one below it, each successive impact closer and louder, giving way to gravity and looking to crush anything in its path. This time, a pickup truck with a coffee cart caught my attention. Again, I considered getting under the truck and cart for cover, and again, I took one step in that direction but diverted at the last moment to continue east down the block.

I was young and fast, but there was no outrunning this monster. Mere seconds later, I was completely lost in darkness. It's as if someone just flicked off the light switch. No more bright sun, no more clouds, just pitch black. The debris storm was a complete assault on my senses, deafening and suffocating at the same time. I ran with my right arm extended outward while my left hand held the top of my shirt close around my mouth and nose. My eyes, nose, and mouth were instantly filled with thick pulverized concrete and other particles. Just as the cloud overtook me, I was surrounded by large chunks of falling debris. As darkness set in all around me, debris was still falling, so I kept running.

I tripped, I fell, and I even ran into parked vehicles. For the record, I do not recommend doing that, ever. But I pressed on into the darkness to escape the kill zone. Each second felt like an eternity, chaos in slow motion. But it was probably mere seconds before I was clear of the falling debris, so I began to walk. I guess stagger would be more accurate. I was clear of the kill zone, but the darkness remained. I could not see, and I could barely breathe. I needed light. I think we all do.

Whispering aloud, I said, "Jesus, help me!" It was all I could muster.

It was enough.

CHAPTER 6

FOLLOW THE LIGHT

I am the light of the world. Whoever follows me will
not walk in darkness, but will have the light of life.
—John 8:12

1001 HOURS, SEPTEMBER 11, 2001, VESEY STREET NEAR BROADWAY, NEW YORK CITY

Jesus is always enough. I staggered forward and saw the strangest thing from the corner of my left eye. I saw light. Follow the light. Oddly, while surrounded by death, when I saw the light, I felt a sense of salvation. For the first time, I was hopeful. Looking back today, this was a moment of clarity that I had a valiant purpose and fierce heart. I believe as I stood in the alley staring at the light, a courageous life of God-ordained mission and meaning was beginning!

I stumbled across the street to realize I was looking north, peering up a very narrow alley. On the opposite end of the alley was sunlight. I immediately began to enter the alley, when the Lord stopped me in my tracks. I didn't realize that to be the case at the time. But I stopped just long enough to hear the voices. What voices do you ask? The painful voices of broken people calling out into the darkness. The debris cloud seemed to suffocate all the sound in the area. But it could not quiet the cries of injured people looking for a way out. Unseen voices calling out into the darkness. They were screaming things like:

"I can't see. Someone help me."

"Please help me. I'm hurt."

"Please help me. Oh God, help me!"

Time to do the next thing. So, for reasons I did not understand at the time, I stood in the mouth of the alley and yelled. I screamed into the darkness, "Follow the sound of my voice. There's light this way! Follow my voice! Follow me to the light!" I repeated this over and over again for several minutes.

Slowly, over time, people made their way to me, and I directed them up the alley toward the light. I wasn't saving the world, but I was doing the next thing. Sometimes, that's all we can do. I was trying to be a beacon in the darkness to bring the injured to the sunlight. Real simple. Just doing the next thing.

Time to Get Serious

I know what you're thinking: *Darin, this story isn't serious enough?* Frankly, no, it's not. This story is simply one of survival in an intense circumstance. I would like to speak now about a far more important story. A story of salvation! Trust me: it's a much bigger deal.

As the tenth anniversary of 9/11 approached, the Lord began to work on my heart. I felt his nudging to begin sharing my 9/11 story in an effort to somehow bring glory to God. When we ignore God's nudges, sometimes, he shoves. He shoved. I was asked by my pastor to share my story with the men of our church at our annual men's BBQ event. At that point, only a dozen or so people in the world knew of my story. It was limited to close friends and family members because the pain was just too much to bear.

I prayed about the invitation and sought counsel from godly men and women in my life. It became clear to me it was time to share my experience in a way that brought glory to God and maybe even introduce some people to the love of Jesus Christ for the first time. That revelation was step one in obedience. This book is step 743 in the process.

Anyway, in preparation for the event, I began to relive the experience frame by frame in my mind. When I got to this point in the story, the scales fell from my eyes. There it was—a beautiful spiritual metaphor hiding in plain sight. The light. Go to the light! I wept. God gave me the first glimpse of how my story could be used to share bigger story. I was humbled and amazed. In an instant, God revealed how He can take even the worst things in life and make them redeemable. I instantly found purpose in telling my story.

Broken in the Desert

I have a great friend named Brian. He has been a mentor to me in many ways. Brian has a great story to tell. Brian was a young man who had the world by the balls. He was a Division I college athlete who competed professionally in Europe for a bit. Then he became an officer in the United States Army, stationed in Europe as a forward artillery officer. Not long after, his world turned upside down. This really bad guy named Saddam Hussein invaded Kuwait, threatening the world's oil supply and stability in the Middle East. Not long after, Brian found himself in the Saudi Arabian desert, preparing to go to war.

As you may remember, the coalition forces initiated a long air campaign named Operation Desert Shield. After five months of moving forces into position and forty days of aerial bombardment, it was time to launch the ground assault to eject Iraqi forces from Kuwait. The ground invasion was phase two of the war, called Operation Desert Storm. It was the night before Brian's unit was to enter Iraq to begin the ground offensive. Brian had been fully briefed by his intelligence officer on what to expect. What he learned had him fearful for himself personally and his men going into combat. Now, today, we all know the ground offensive of Desert Storm was a rout. So even though his unit suffered almost fifty casualties, the Iraqi forces were decimated in Kuwait with minimal US casualties.

But that was not the expectation. The casualty projections provided to Brian were haunting. The intelligence suggested Brian could lose up to 30 percent of his 1,200 troops. In his mind, he was about to lead his men into combat, and many would not survive.

So, he took a walk in the desert.

Brian was overcome with darkness and doom. He was lost and scared. He even recorded his last will and testament on an audio recorder. Brian did not believe in God and the power of Jesus's death and resurrection. But he cried out anyway. And God answered. God always answers.

God spoke to Brian in the desert night, much like he did to Abraham centuries earlier. He told Brian, "Let my light in!" Boom! My dear friend Brian dropped to his knees in the Saudi Arabian desert and declared Jesus as his Lord and Savior. And as Brian tells it, he went to bed and slept peacefully.

And would you believe Brian entered combat at 4:00 a.m. the next day with zero fear in his heart? He was ready to rain down artillery hell on the enemy because he knew he would be saving the lives of the brothers he loved. Brian didn't search within himself and muster up the courage to lead his men. He also didn't "fake it till you make it" either.

He simply invited the God of light and salvation into his heart, and his fear was obliterated.

God's perfect love casts out all fear (1 John 4:18). Jesus did the work, and Brian just followed. Today, Brian uses a beautiful illustration as he retells his story. He says, at that time in his life, he was doing everything *he* could do to rid his life of darkness and fear. He equates it to entering a dark room, opening a window, and trying to shovel out the darkness from the room. But as Brian explains, it doesn't work that way. In order to see in the dark room, you gotta bring in the "Light!"

The Bridge to Cross

If you are a believer in Jesus Christ, then I want this chapter to act as a reminder of whom you serve. But more importantly, this section is for the reader who does *not* know Jesus as Lord. Allow me to introduce you to the Light of the World.

As a Christian, I believe that God created the world, and it was perfect, but only for a short time (Genesis 1 and 2). Sin was brought into the world by Adam's rebellion and passivity. From that time forward, there was a schism between God, Who is holy, and mankind, who is unholy. The sin of man is the source of all pain, suffering, and brokenness in the world (Genesis 3).

The Old Testament of the Bible is the story of God's chosen people, the Jews, and His attempts to reconcile the Creator with the created. Time and again, God's people are given instructions and commandments to follow. Sometimes, even for generations, God's people follow in the ways of the Lord and are blessed. But eventually, His people fall short (every time) and turn away from the Lord, even to other gods and idols.

The Old Testament is full of wisdom and paints a beautiful portrait of who God is and why He is worthy of our praise. The Old Testament is where we learn the true character and faithfulness of God. But most importantly, the Old Testament overwhelmingly illuminates the dire need for a savior. Man, who is unholy despite his best efforts, can never again dwell in the presence of God, Who is perfectly holy. The Scriptures reveal there must be a bridge to connect the two sides. That bridge is Jesus Christ. And that bridge can now be crossed by Jews, gentiles (non-Jews), and all God's children. That includes you!

The Light of Life

John 8:12 records this proclamation from Jesus: "I am the light of the world. Whoever follows me will not walk in darkness but will have the light of life." The Lord has put a multifaceted, valiant purpose in my heart. Part of that purpose is to introduce nonbelievers to the power, awe, majesty, and fierce love of Jesus.

You see, sin is an act that carries a penalty. A penalty that creates a debt that must be paid. The ultimate penalty to be paid is death, for the wages of sin is death (Romans 6:23).

Christians believe the God of the Bible is both a God of Love and a God of Justice. Only God, through the sacrifice of Jesus Christ, can be 100 percent both at the same time. Story time, boys and girls. A former pastor and good friend of mine, Tony Hinchliff, once used this childlike illustration to explain the concept:

There once was a young prince who became the king of his kingdom. Life was good in the kingdom, and he was a trusted and admired king. But over time, corruption began to take root in the kingdom. The young king vowed to find those responsible and bring them to justice. In due time, the king discovered that his very own mother was the source of corruption in the kingdom.

The king and his subjects were shocked. The law of the land called for this crime to be punished by receiving lashings while tied to a post. The young king was in a very precarious situation, and his people knew it. If he punished his own mother for the crime, then how could he possibly be viewed as a loving king? If he let his mother escape from the sentence, then how could he claim to be a just king?

The morning of the punishment arrived. Just as the king's mother was about to be tied to the post, the king stepped forward. Quietly, he removed his robe, tied himself to the post, and instructed the lashings to begin—on *his* back. This was a true king. He was loving, and he was just. A ransom was required, and *he* paid it. The perfect balance of justice and love. The young king in the story is Jesus of Nazareth.

Now it's not a perfect illustration, but I think it's a great way to view the love and justice of God. In a cold stable in Bethlehem, over two thousand years ago, the greatest rescue mission of all time was launched. Jesus, the Son of God, humbled himself by coming to the earth in the form of a man (Philippians 2:7). He lived a full life, being 100 percent man and 100 percent God. He lived what we lived and experienced what we experienced. Jesus knew hurt, loneliness, hunger, pain, and suffering. He also experienced love, laughter, and joy. And when the time came, He answered the bell! He submitted himself to His father's will. He submitted himself to death, even death on a cross (Philippians 2:8).

Remember: the penalty of sin is death, meaning eternal separation from God. But Jesus took the sins of mankind (past, present, and future) onto himself. He who knew no sin, became sin itself (2 Corinthians 5:21) so that you and I may have life. Jesus took the full wrath of God onto himself so that you and I could become righteous before his eyes. The gap has been bridged. All you need to do is walk across the bridge into the light!

The Light, Jesus living in your soul, is available to you right now. And it doesn't cost you a thing. It's a free gift called grace. In Ephesians 2, the apostle Paul declares that before Christ, we were all "sons of disobedience" and "children of wrath." But God, Paul writes, being rich in mercy and love, brings us to life through the atoning death of Jesus Christ. This passage makes it clear that we are saved not by works (good behavior/deeds) but rather by our faith alone through God's grace alone.

Grace is God's unmerited or undeserved favor upon us by the actions of Jesus, not us. Then, and only then, will you experience contentment, fulfillment, and lasting joy. Sounds like a sweet deal, right? Look, this world is a dark place. Let's be honest: it's not really getting any better either. Sadness, depression, loneliness, anxiety, anger, and fear rule the day. I think we have enough of that in the world. How about some light? Jesus, the Light of the World, offers peace, joy, contentment, and real life! Colossians 1:13 says, "He has delivered us from the domain of darkness and transferred us to the kingdom of his beloved Son."

Go to the Light

Now back to my illustration. There I was, standing in the mouth of the alley, calling people to the light. What a beautiful spiritual metaphor. To be clear, that is not what I was thinking at the time. But now I see the illustration for what it is—a valiant call to lead people out of the darkness into the arms of King Jesus. Like I said before, maybe fifteen or so people made their way to me in that alley. I think it is worth mentioning something else here. And that's the condition of the people as they approached me on that "battlefield." They looked much like I did. They were beaten and bloodied. Scarred and bruised. Filthy from head to toe. Here, our illustration continues. Because that is the *exact* condition of all of us when we initially turn to Christ! We are walking in darkness, scarred and wounded, covered in the filth of our own sin.

And please hear this. In this condition, Jesus doesn't turn up his nose, give the stop sign with his hand, and say, "You are a broken, filthy mess. Go clean yourself up first!" Nope. If that were the case, then *none* of us could ever approach Jesus. Because the fact is we all mess up and fall short of the glory of God (Romans 3:23). The truth is Jesus takes us as we are right now. He doesn't insist we get perfect first or master some sin we have always wrestled with. He takes us as we are, and *then* He starts knocking down walls in our hearts and busting strongholds in our souls.

You will find strength and an inner peace that knows no bounds. I promise! Go to the light! You will never perish, and you will spend eternity in the presence of God because Jesus has ransomed and rescued you. The Bible is very clear. If you confess with your mouth that Jesus is Lord and you believe in your heart that God raised him from the dead, then you will be saved (Romans 10:9). In other words, you just have to truly believe the biblical account of Jesus and say it out loud. That's it. Then you are taken from the domain of darkness and ushered into the kingdom of light.

Go to the light!

CHAPTER 7

BE THE LIGHT

You are the light of the world ... Let your light shine
before others, so that they may see your good works
and give glory to your father who is in heaven.
—Matthew 5:14–16

1002 HOURS, SEPTEMBER 11, 2001, VESEY STREET NEAR BROADWAY, NEW YORK CITY

So, there I stood, in the mouth of the alley, shouting at the top of my injured lungs, "Follow the sound of my voice!" I repeated that desperate call, or something like it, over and over. "Come this way. There is light! There is a way out! Follow the sound of my voice. Come this way!"

Slowly, approximately ten to fifteen injured and lost people found me in the darkness. I assessed each one for major injuries and then sent them up the alley toward the sunlight. Oddly, we hardly spoke a word. One by one, the nameless victims trudged north, hopefully to safer ground. Eventually, I turned to head up the alley myself.

Only now, the sunlight was gone.

Cries were emanating out of the darkness from the broken and lost. For me, it's an unforgettable moment in my story. Those cries were answered in some small way by me. But I would argue that this scene parallels much of our modern world. Except the cries I'm speaking of are answered for eternity by the King and Kings and the Lord of Lords. Jesus said, "I am the way, and the truth, and the life; no one comes to the Father except through me" (John 14:6). And he calls on his followers to be his ambassadors to the world.

To my brothers and sisters in Christ, this is part of our calling. Consider this a challenge to the universal Church, specifically the American evangelical church. Here is your mission if you choose to accept it. Be the man or woman standing in the alley, pointing people to King Jesus. It really is that simple. In the previous chapter, I mentioned this passage from Ephesians 2.

And you were dead in the trespasses and sins in which you once walked, following the course of this world, following the prince of the power of the air, the spirit that is now at work in the sons of disobedience; among whom we all once lived in the passions of our flesh, carrying out the desires of the body and the mind, and were by nature children of wrath, like the rest of mankind. But God, being rich in mercy, because of the great love with which he loved us, even when we were dead in our trespasses, made us alive together with Christ—by grace you have been saved—and raised us up with him in the heavenly places in Christ Jesus, so that in the coming ages he might show the immeasurable riches of his grace and kindness toward us in Christ Jesus. For by grace you have been saved through faith. And this is not of your own doing; it is a gift of God, not a result of works, so that no one may boast. For we are his workmanship, created in Christ Jesus for good works, which God prepared beforehand, that we should walk in them. (Ephesians 2:1–10)

In my opinion, Ephesians 2:1–10 is a beautiful encapsulation of the Christian gospel. It can be summed up this way.

1. Who we were before Christ: dead to sin, sons of disobedience, and children of wrath.
2. Who we were after accepting Jesus: alive with Christ and seated with Him in the heavenly places.
3. Now what? What do we do with this grace through faith that has saved us?

Universal Purpose

Ephesians 2:10 states, "For we are his workmanship, created in Christ Jesus for good works, which God prepared beforehand, that we should walk in them." We were saved for a reason and that reason is to do the good works which God has laid before us. The original Greek word in the text for "workmanship" can be translated to "masterpiece."

This means that each one of us is uniquely and perfectly designed for a specific purpose, a valiant purpose. God designed you, and only you, to boldly live out His will for your life in the cause of advancing His kingdom. We will carefully unpack this concept of personal calling in part IV of this book. But for now, I want to focus on a universal purpose that binds all Christians together. It's called the Great Commission.

Jesus spoke in Matthew 28:18–19:

And Jesus came up and spoke to them, saying, "All authority in heaven and on earth has been given to Me. Go, therefore, and make disciples of all the nations, baptizing them in the name of the Father and the Son and the Holy Spirit."

Regardless of who you are and where you live. If you are a believer in Jesus, then you share in this great mission to *go* and make disciples of all nations. Where Jesus is not known, there is darkness. And just like my friend Brian said, you cannot push the darkness from existence. You must bring in the light. And that light is Jesus, the light of the world. And whoever follows Jesus, will never walk in darkness again, but will have life (John 8:12). Real life. This is called evangelism, and it is the will of God. Paul writes in 1 Timothy 2:3–4:

This is good and acceptable in the sight of God our Savior, who wants all people to be saved and to come to the knowledge of the truth.

The Bible commands believers to serve as "witnesses" and "ambassadors." Therefore, as Christians, it is our universally shared purpose to do one of two things: point people to the light or be a representation of the light in this dark world.

You Will Be My Witnesses

First, let's talk about pointing people to the light by being a "witness for Christ." In Acts 1:8, the resurrected Jesus gives the following command to his disciples: "But you will receive power when the Holy Spirit has come upon you, and you will be my witnesses in Jerusalem and in all Judea and Samaria, and to the ends of the earth."

Think about what it means to be a witness in a trial of law. In a court proceeding, a witness testifies to two simple things. They testify to what they have seen and what they know. In regard to being the light of Christ in this world, we simply need to share what we have seen Jesus do and what we know is true about Jesus. Many people feel this to be a daunting task and struggle to find a starting point. May I suggest a very simple icebreaker? "Hey, I know you don't necessarily believe in Jesus, but I would love to tell you how he rescued me. Can I share with you my story?" Boom. That's it. You're welcome. You are being a witness by testifying how Jesus has changed your life, what you have seen.

In the previous chapter, I mentioned how my experience on 9/11 was merely a survival story, and that's true. I also alluded to the fact that each Christian holds in their heart a much greater story, one of salvation. Just tell people your salvation story. Think about it. You were a child of wrath, and now you are an adopted son of the King. That's a big freaking 180-degree turn. Share that. Some of you grew up in a Christian household, learned all the stories, and knew all the songs. Yet, at some juncture, you reached a decision point. Is this stuff real or not? And you chose: real. So just explain that process and, more importantly, describe what God has done in your life since saying yes to Jesus.

Others of you may have a more dramatic experience to share. A story of hitting rock bottom, maybe some kind of addiction or traumatic incident. Yet Jesus loved you, sought you, called you by name, and you answered Him. Your story can be a powerful force in leading someone out of the darkness and into the light.

But your story is useless if you do not share it. Useless.

God didn't create you to be useless. When telling your story, it's also important to emphasize you are now forever a child of God. Jesus died for your past and present sins, and also your future sins. Yes, unfortunately, we will all continue to sin. But believe me, Jesus knew what he was purchasing when he paid the price. He didn't make a mistake. As we share our story, we must emphasize that we are now forever His. Jesus said in John 10:27–28, "My sheep hear my voice and I know them and they follow me. I give them eternal life and they will never perish, and no one will snatch them from my hand." Your story matters. Share it. Use it as a vessel to point people to Jesus.

The Scriptures also make clear Christians are to be a representation of Jesus in the world. We are called to be different and walk in a manner that is worthy of the Lord (Colossians 1:10). In the words of Jesus in Matthew 5:14–16:

> You are the light of the world. A city set on a hill cannot be hidden. Nor do people light a lamp and put it under a basket, but on a stand, so it gives light to all in the house. In the same way, *let your light shine before others* [my emphasis], so that they may see your good works and give glory to your Father in heaven.

Are you letting your light shine before others? We agree that in order to pierce the darkness, we must bring in the light. According to Scripture, it would appear sometimes that light is you! Are you an agent of light in your sphere of influence? By "sphere of influence," I mean anywhere your presence is known and it carries weight. Examples might be your family, workplace, community, neighborhood, or school and in your friendships. Do people know you as simply a nice person, or do they *know* you are a redeemed believer who takes God and His Word seriously?

Ambassadors in an Unholy Land

The Bible also refers to Christians as "ambassadors for Christ." The apostle Paul writes in 2 Corinthians 5:19, "That is in Christ, God was reconciling the world to himself . . . and entrusting to us the message of reconciliation." Simply stated, God is holy, and we are not. God brought us into holiness through Christ alone, not because of our awesomeness. We are now reconciled to, or have made peace with, God. Then God bestows possibly the most humbling honor onto his believers. He entrusts us to help deliver this inconceivable message of reconciliation to the world.

Continuing in 2 Corinthians 5:20, Paul goes on to say, "Therefore, we are ambassadors for Christ, God making his appeal through us. We implore you, on behalf of Christ, to be reconciled to God." Whoa, wait a minute! The God of all creation. The God Who simply spoke the world into existence. The God Who is all things and above all things. That God wants to use you and me to deliver His message of redemption to the world. This simply blows my mind. But why do I and so many other Christians often ignore this assignment? Because it seems too difficult or we believe the lie that we are not worthy messengers. That would be true if we had to rely only upon ourselves for our good standing before a holy God. But the Scriptures are clear. We are brought into good standing (reconciled) with God only because of the redemption offered by Jesus and his resurrection. By faith, through grace. Therefore, we *can* be his ambassadors in a foreign land.

I know a little about ambassadors and foreign lands. In my Secret Service career, I had the honor of serving in forty different countries. Sometimes, they were short assignments, only lasting days. Other times, they were weeks. Sometimes, we were guests of a friendly nation, and sometimes, not so much. One of my longest assignments was over a month in Lisbon, Portugal. I was part of a very sensitive investigative case involving a vast criminal enterprise. It was extremely complex and required meticulous cooperation with Portuguese law enforcement organizations. My team and I were under strict orders from the ambassador of the United States to Portugal, and the orders were don't screw up relations in my backyard.

And it was made very clear, on day one, that there was a one voice policy toward the Portuguese government. And that voice was that of the US Ambassador, no one else. The message did not need clarification. "Do your job, know your role, and leave the talking to me." That's because the US ambassador in any given country is the lone voice representing the United States. This is what an ambassador does. They live in a foreign land, and they speak for a higher authority. Such is the mindset that we, as Christians, must embrace as "ambassadors for Christ." We courageously live in a foreign land, and we boldly represent a higher authority.

Early in my career, I was operating in a foreign country

that was officially "friendly" toward the United States. Not really, though. This place was evil, and we walked with targets on our backs. But on day one of the assignment, the US ambassador looked the three of us in the eye and said, "If you get taken, I will come get you." I believed him. Not because he was some double-tough special ops guy. He wasn't. I believed him because I knew he could wield power far greater than himself. He had the weight of the entire US government behind him if he needed it.

Christians, not only do we represent a higher authority, but we also have the power of the one true God behind us. "Finally, be strong in the Lord and in the strength of His might" (Ephesians 6:10). Therefore, we are able to walk in a manner worthy of the Lord. We bring the light of Christ into the darkness. We let our light shine before men. It's a spiritual war, and your community is your battlefield. Will you enter the fight? Will you answer the bell? We deliver the message, the gospel, of Jesus to a foreign land in desperate need of a savior. We are His witnesses. That's what it means to be an ambassador, standing in the alley, as possibly the lone voice, pointing people to Jesus. Will you be that ambassador?

PART II

THE OPPOSITE OF FEAR

CHAPTER 8

TELL ME WHY

Theirs is not to reason why, theirs but to do and die.
Into the valley of Death rode the six hundred.
—Alfred Lord Tennyson, *The Charge of the Light Brigade*

APPROXIMATELY 1008 HOURS, SEPTEMBER 11, 2001, VESEY STREET NEAR BROADWAY, NEW YORK CITY

Quiet. Darkness. Indecision. Standing in the mouth of the nameless alley, there was a lull in the action, with minuscule movement on the street. The thick cloud still hung in the air. The street was covered with dust and ash. So much so that they blanketed all noise, even my footfalls on the concrete were muffled.

I was uncertain of my next move. Did I stay on the scene, or did I evacuate the area? I was also alone. I'm a social person who loves connecting with people, so I've never been fond of solitude. But especially on this day, I hated being alone. I needed my brothers, and I needed a plan. But at that moment, my body needed to settle down. My eyes and lungs needed a reprieve from the elements, so I began to look for shelter. I decided to head north up the alley toward the light.

But as I turned around, I was punched in the gut by reality. The light was gone. Replaced only by a gray soup of ash and pulverized concrete. Onward into the darkness, I trudged.

I staggered north up the alley in an attempt to escape the debris storm for fresh air.

I didn't make it all the way to the end. Not far up the alley, I noticed a sudden movement to my right. I was not alone.

Through the gloom, I could see a set of terror-filled eyes staring at me through a crack in a slightly ajar door. Shelter and a companion. I approached the door as the set of eyes disappeared from view. Slowly, I opened the door to find a small storage room attached to one of the shops on the block. It was almost pitch black inside but the air was measurably more breathable. Inside the room were my two new best friends. The eyes I had seen belonged to a small Russian woman with a heavy accent named Anna. The other was a tall, thin bearded man. We didn't exchange names. For some reason, he never offered. Probably because he was calm and composed while Anna was in a state of panic. I closed the door to prevent the debris from polluting the air in our small refuge. When I did so, the room had zero ambient light, sending Anna into more of a frenzy.

Now, this would have been a great time for my flashlight. You know, the one thing the Secret Service trained me to *always* have on my person. The one I neglected to grab when I retrieved other useless gear from my desk. Yeah, that one. Pro tip, free of charge, on the house: every man should always carry a small flashlight clipped to their shorts/pants pocket. It will possibly save your life in an emergency, or (much more likely) it will keep you from stepping on Lego pieces in bare feet while exiting your kid's dark bedroom at bedtime. Have you ever stepped on a Lego with bare feet? It's worse than waterboarding. You will use the flashlight all the time—trust me. You're welcome.

As if this scene couldn't get stranger, out of nowhere, Anna produced an old cheap disposable film camera. I put my hand on her shoulder and asked if I could have the camera. She complied, and I backed away.

"Look, watch this. Relax," I told her. I pointed the camera in all four directions, taking a picture each time. With each flash of the camera bulb, a short burst of light illuminated the confines of our tiny refuge. Anna immediately calmed down. My guess is the trauma of the situation pushed this young woman to revert back to being a little girl. She was scared of the dark.

It's interesting what bringing a little light can do.

We stayed in the room for about ten minutes until the debris cloud outside began to slowly dissipate. Oddly enough, the tall, thin bearded man barely spoke the entire time. He seemed to become invisible during Anna's period of distress. He stood silently off to the side and had occasionally peeked out the door to examine the conditions in the alley. He was steady, a picture of calm in the storm.

We all decided it was time to leave our refuge and head north to safety. As we exited the room, I directed them up the alley, out of the danger zone, away from the WTC site.

"Are you not coming with us?" asked Anna.

"I'm going back" was my curt reply. The bearded man was kind enough to hand me his handkerchief to wrap around my face, protecting my lungs from the lingering debris particles. It proved to be very helpful, as I wore it for the remainder of the day. I wished them well, and then Anna asked a question. A question for which I still don't have an answer.

"Why is this happening?" she asked. Ugh. What a gut punch. I had no idea how to respond.

Searching for the answer myself, I quietly asked, "Do you believe in God?"

"Yes!" she replied but quickly followed with, "But why would God let this happen?"

Ouch. Talk about a one-two punch combination!

Theirs Is Not to Reason Why

Why would God let an event like 9/11 happen? More broadly, why would an all-powerful, all-knowing, and all-loving God allow any pain and suffering in the world?

I'll start with a brief answer and then add some context. My answer to the more specific question is I don't know. And I believe anyone who tries to definitively tell you exactly why God allowed 9/11 to happen is a fool. I do know that on this side of eternity, we can't make sense of much of the world around us. But one day, those who call Jesus their Lord and Savior will see all things clearly. The Bible says this much in the beautiful words written by the apostle Paul: "For now we see in a mirror dimly, but then face to face. Now I know in part; then I shall know fully, even as I have been fully known" (1 Corinthians 13:12).

I also take solace and comfort in the promises of God surrounding the unanswered questions of life, one being, "For my thoughts are not your thoughts, neither are your ways my ways, declares the Lord. For as the heavens are higher than the earth, so are my ways higher than your ways and my thoughts higher than your thoughts" (Isaiah 55: 8–9).

God is the Creator of the universe. He is the beginning and the end, the Alpha and the Omega. It is only reasonable to accept that I (as a flawed created being) will not always be able to comprehend the ways/thoughts of God, the Creator.

Now, let's address the larger question: Why does God allow pain and suffering in this world? I understand this question is a massive stumbling block for many, even keeping some from saving faith. I am very comfortable in knowing my own limitations and providing a sound argument for this issue is one of them. I will not attempt here to make a case on this issue when others have already done so brilliantly, far beyond my ability. Specifically, Pastor Tim Keller comes to mind.

Timothy Keller was one of the most prominent theologians and pastors of our time. Ironically, he pastored a church, Redeemer New York, just blocks from the World Trade Center. Keller brilliantly tackles this issue in his 2008 book *The Reason for God*. It's a modern masterpiece. He addresses this question in chapter 2. I strongly encourage readers, believers and nonbelievers, to read his work as you wrestle with this issue. One can summarize one of Keller's key points as follows: Christianity may not provide a specific reason for pain and suffering. But that doesn't mean God doesn't love us. God chose to come down to our world with the explicit goal of taking all our pain and suffering upon himself on the cross. Through Jesus, God experienced all of our pain and suffering and then some.

With that fact in mind, I'll also quote Peter Kreeft: "Therefore, though Christianity does not provide the reason for each pain, it provides deep resources for actually facing suffering with hope and courage rather than bitterness and despair."[1] I highly encourage you to read Keller's *The Reason for God*.

1   Peter Kreeft, *Making Sense Out of Suffering* (St. Anthony Messenger Press, 1986).

You will be a better human being for it.

But Anna wanted an answer now. "But why would God let this happen?" This is it. This is my moment. A beautiful story of saving grace found in tragic loss is about to happen. My brilliant answer will no doubt instantly bring Anna to the point of saving faith, right? Well, not so much. I'm honestly embarrassed by my reply. I've always thought of my answer as weak, impotent, or lame. Or is it?

I put my hand on her shoulder and said, "I don't know, Anna, but we must believe God is good." Anna began to weep. I know my answer didn't solve her dilemma, but she seemed encouraged as she wiped away her tears. God is good. God is love. These truths powered me the remainder of the day. Sometimes, faith requires worship even in the darkness.

APPROXIMATELY 1018 HOURS, SEPTEMBER 11, 2001, VESEY STREET NEAR BROADWAY, NEW YORK CITY

There was no time to dwell on my final interaction with Anna. She and the bearded man headed north for safety. Meanwhile, I pursued the chaos. Time to make some good trouble. Walking south, I quickly reached the mouth of the alley. I took a right turn, back in the direction of the WTC site. As I approached the next intersection, the debris cloud had mostly cleared. Unfortunately, in its place was blood, panic, and destruction. I witnessed the entire spectrum of the human condition. Violence. Chaos. Madness. Kindness. Acts of compassion. That's how I would describe the scene in front of me. I was about to come face to face with utter human tragedy while at the same time having a front-row seat to the power of love. Two extremes, one scene.

I stood motionless for a few moments as I processed my surroundings. People, injured and uninjured, were scurrying all about. The wounded walked slowly, seemingly dazed and confused. No doubt their bodies had already gone into shock. The uninjured ones hastily moved around, trying to assist the wounded or make sense of the scene themselves. And then it happened. A wounded man staggered across the street, oblivious to his surroundings. Simultaneously, an FDNY ambulance careened around the corner as it rushed to the scene. The ambulance driver slammed on the brakes, but it was too late.

The large vehicle plowed into the dazed pedestrian, sending him flying through the air only to land in a crumpled heap.

The ambulance came to a screeching halt, and the FDNY members began life-saving measures. On a normal day, one might sit and gawk at an accident such as this. But this was no ordinary day. Immediately, I saw a person attempting to walk toward me on the sidewalk. I say person because, oddly, I cannot remember if it was a man or a woman. Possibly, it was because I was focused on the broken leg bone sticking out of his or her skin. This person, no doubt in shock, was attempting to walk with a compound leg fracture. I gently picked him/her up to carry to an ambulance down the block. A man ran away as he saw my struggle and soon returned with a shopping cart. We carefully placed the victim into the cart, and my unknown partner pushed the injured person down the block to waiting first responders.

The scene before me was tragic and awe-inspiring at the same time. The destruction and walking wounded combined to create an apocalyptic landscape of pain and suffering.

However, there was beauty to behold among the madness. I witnessed a community instantly banding together for the greater good. It's worth noting that just a couple of blocks away, a 110-level skyscraper had just collapsed. Yet these people, untrained civilians, didn't run like most. They stayed. They chose to answer the bell. They sacrificed their own comfort and safety for the sake of their fellow citizens. This is the best of America.

I witnessed victims tending to each other's wounds. Citizens poured out from bodegas and drug stores with arms full of first aid medical supplies. I witnessed citizens gathering food and water to distribute to those in need. I vividly remember a large man standing on the corner. Over each shoulder, he carried a five-gallon water jug. Those things are heavy. People stood in line in front of him, each stepping forward to take a drink. I waited patiently. When it was my turn, I tilted the jug toward my face but didn't drink a drop. I just flushed my eyes, ears, and face of the debris and soot. I was wet and filthy, but for the first time in a while, I could see clearly. With clear eyes, it was time to get back in the fight.

I guess I made a decision, except I don't remember making it or even considering the options. Perhaps I just zombie-walked down the street. More likely, the Spirit led me to where I was needed. Regardless, I was standing on the southwest corner of Church Street and Vesey Street. That's right. I had planted myself in the same intersection from which my mad dash for survival had begun. I had returned to the scene of the crime.

I scanned the area, desperately checking faces, looking for "my guys." And I found one. Finally, a familiar face. His name was Frank Larkin, and he was a supervisor in my office. Frank was a highly respected boss, known for leading by example. This is all you need to know about Frank: long before joining the US Secret Service, Frank was a US Navy SEAL. I worked with him for years and never knew he was a SEAL. If I were ever a SEAL, I would find a way to work that into my introduction to anyone I met. Who doesn't want to brag about being a SEAL? Well, Frank Larkin, for one. Frank is a man of genuine humility.

But our reunion didn't last long. As we stood there and talked about our next move, I heard a strange sound, a familiar sound. It was a high-pitched screeching noise resembling metal scratching on metal. The steel beams of WTC Tower 1 were about to lose their battle with burning jet fuel and gravity.

We had only seconds to spare. Time to run. Again.

CHAPTER 9

CITIZENS OF A REPUBLIC

There is little use for the being whose tepid soul knows nothing of the great and generous emotion, of the high pride, the stern belief, the lofty enthusiasm, of the men who quell the storm and ride the thunder.
—Theodore Roosevelt, *Citizenship in a Republic*

1028 HOURS, SEPTEMBER 11, 2001, CORNER OF CHURCH STREET AND VESEY STREET, NEW YORK CITY

Surely, the sky wouldn't fall twice on the same day, right? Looking back, there was a stark contrast between the scenes on the ground when each tower collapsed. Earlier, when WTC 2 fell, the street was covered with civilians dressed in business attire. They walked crookedly and slowly away from the scene, awkwardly looking up at the burning buildings. Then they frantically ran as the tower tumbled to the ground. This time, however, almost all people on the street were first responders. They were scurrying around with heads down, moving with purpose while "working the problem." But just prior to the collapse, everyone heard what I heard. And we all knew the lights were about to go out again.

So, we got a head start. I pivoted off my right foot and began to sprint with Frank right beside me. I probably made it about ten to fifteen seconds before hearing the first thunderclap. It was loud but gratefully more distant than my first experience. I knew I had a chance. This time, I dashed north (instead of east) up Church Street. The ground I earned quickly began to evaporate behind me as the "thunder" rolled to a crescendo up my back. I decided to turn right, and Frank kept going straight. We became separated in our mad dash for life.

I planted my left foot into the asphalt and turned hard right down an unidentified street. I was in trouble, and I knew it. My evasive action didn't shake my pursuer. Legs and lungs churning, I was burning through my third adrenaline dump of the day. But I was about to be consumed again. I took another hard right turn, and in desperation, I plowed my right shoulder into the opening of a revolving door. My world momentarily spun as the door churned and spit me out on the other side. I fell flat on my back, slamming my head to the marble floor. I lowered my chin just in time to see the debris storm devour the street outside. I exhaled. Refuge.

I stared at the ceiling for a few moments as I tried to catch my breath. After a couple minutes, I heard the swoosh as the revolving door made another revolution. I didn't pay attention to the two haggard men as they stumbled in. But then it happened. The words are still clear in my mind: "Kinder, is that you?"

"Thank you, Jesus," I muttered to myself. I was fighting the good fight, and in return, He had provided not only shelter from the storm but also wind in my sails. The "wind" was my guys. I was immediately energized. I rolled over, pushed up to my knees, raised my eyes, and said, "Oh, hey, guys." Two Secret Service brothers, Rob Donovan and John Beck (a different John from before) were staring down at me from above. They looked very similar to me—beaten, bloodied, and tattered clothes. They, too, had chosen to be in the fight. I was not surprised because it matched their character. They helped me up, and we exchanged hugs.

After assessing the situation, we began to plan our next move. We decided, as one, to answer the bell. Several other civilians in the lobby joined us in the center of the room. Rob, John, and I, with the others, knew our day was not done. Collectively, we planned to wait in our little refuge for ten to fifteen minutes to allow the debris cloud to dissipate slightly. Once minimum visibility was established, we divided into two groups and deployed into the gloom.

APPROXIMATELY 1050 HOURS, SEPTEMBER 11, 2001, CHURCH STREET, JUST NORTH OF WTC SITE, NEW YORK CITY

The suffocating blanket of dust and debris particles had returned. Therefore, we walked in eerie silence. The sun was blotted from the sky, replaced by a gray soup, air so thick you could taste it. The smell of smoke and death competed with each other for supremacy. The scene was apocalyptic. We divided ourselves into two groups with a shared mission: find the wounded and bring them to emergency care. "Once more into the fray, into the last great fight I'll ever know."

We searched for wounded but only found bodies.

It hurts to write that sentence, but that was our result. Each group bumbled through the haze, intentionally staying within earshot since visibility was less than fifteen feet.

Suddenly, I heard Rob cry out, "We got one!"

Their group emerged from the fog, and we led them back to the lobby of our shelter. The victim was an unconscious adult male not responding to stimuli. Rob or John, I can't remember which, began preparing to provide CPR, but it was quickly deduced the victim was already gone, deceased. Everyone was quiet. To my recollection, not a word was said. One person stayed with the body as the two groups once more returned to the street.

We slowly worked our way back toward the intersection of Church and Vesey streets. Along the way, we realized we were ill-equipped for our mission. I led my group to the entrance of the massive United States Post Office building located on Church Street. I had an idea and only shared it once we were inside. Desperate times call for desperate measures. We were about to commit a few felonies, even the federal kind. I instructed everyone to spread out, search, and steal (borrow) any equipment we could use in our mission. Our objectives were flashlights, fire extinguishers, first aid kits, AEDs (automated external defibrillators), and the like.

We dispersed and began ransacking (lightly) the post office. Our "search" mostly had negative results. I managed to scavenge a tiny fire extinguisher and another team member inexplicably walked out with a handful of trash bags. Trash bags? Really? Anyway, we pressed on back into the street to continue our search.

The hope of our search was to find survivors. But that hope proved to be short-lived. Along the way, each group stumbled upon several bodies, but none breathing. Later that evening and into the next day, thousands of healthy New

Yorkers would flood into the area hospitals to donate life-saving blood for the victims. But blood was largely unneeded. Rescuers were only finding bodies in the carnage. We experienced the same results, only sooner. In my opinion, that reality did not make our efforts futile. Because still today, I draw strength and inspiration from the citizens who stepped up, entered the fray, and fought the good fight for their fellow man. Citizens, not civilians. There's a difference.

Citizens, Not Civilians

Every man and woman who stepped forward to join our search party was a citizen, not a civilian, full stop. Allow me to explain. A good friend of mine once shared his thoughts on the difference between a civilian and a citizen. His name is Clint Bruce, and he is one of a kind. Clint grew up in Arkansas and Texas, then went on to be an All-American linebacker and team captain at the United States Naval Academy. Clint was a fierce competitor on and off the field. For example, one time, he declared on national television that he was going to bite off his opponent's finger and mail it to his mother. Like I said, fierce. After a stint in the NFL, Clint became a US Navy SEAL where his wartime accomplishments rivaled his football heroics. Today, Clint is a successful entrepreneur and a leader of men in the business world.

Here is the distinction Clint makes. Civilians are consumers of society. They take but rarely give. They are often oblivious to the efforts and sacrifices made in order for their society to flourish. Civilians contribute little to their community, but they sleep peacefully knowing the lights will turn on, the water will run, the trash will be picked up, someone will respond to the 911 calls, and so on.

Since they barely contribute to their community, a civilian is centered on self-preservation. Earlier in my story, I spoke of the people in the WTC stairwell blindly walking past the woman slumped over in the corner. They were civilians. The citizen, as Clint explains, is different. A true citizen is someone who rightly draws from the benefits of society because they have made deposits of their own for the greater good. A citizen is not consumed with self but rather outwardly focused. A citizen protects and nurtures his family because he knows a strong, healthy family will inherit the land and the republic in which they live. A citizen will donate her time to address a societal problem because she cannot ignore pain and suffering in her presence. A citizen's "work time" is not limited to his profession but rather extends into his family, relationships, and community. Anyone can be a civilian, but being a citizen requires noble effort.

In 1910, former US president Theodore Roosevelt gave a famous speech at Sorbonne University in Paris, France. This address is often referred to as the "man in the arena" speech for its rousing call for men to truly live by "daring greatly." However, it was actually titled "Citizenship in a Republic." Throughout the address, Roosevelt powerfully paints a picture of the vital requirements that are laid upon citizens if their republic is to survive. Among other things, Roosevelt states a citizen must have "the will and power to work" so that his family can thrive and the surpluses shared with the greater society. In addition, a citizen should be strong and brave, ready to fight when needed if the fight is righteous.

Roosevelt not only called citizens to action but also encouraged them to take heart even in our failures. According to Roosevelt, pursuing noble ventures with all your heart and strength, that's the stuff of a citizen. In part IV of this book, we will revisit Teddy Roosevelt and his message to citizens. Be ready. There is a unique "arena" waiting for you, and only for you, to enter.

Only the Brave

I'd like to take some time to expand on my friend Clint's civilian/citizen comparison. There are two other smaller groups that follow citizens. Most are not called to these groups, which is good. Because most are not made or wired for these groups. To me, both groups are forever linked to the events of 9/11, and I want to honor them: guardians and warriors. Only the brave need apply. In Plato's *Republic*, he writes of three fundamental "classes" of people that would make up his ideal city-state (society). While I do not agree with much of Plato's ideas for an "ideal" society, I appreciate his basic concept of guardians and warriors.

Guardians are the brave men and women who establish order and deliver justice in their community. Guardians work closely together to keep the peace and ensure an equal application of the law. They protect and preserve the infrastructure upon which a community functions. And they serve their community in times of emergency and despair. In modern times, our guardians are the members of the first responder community: cops, firefighters, emergency medical services personnel. Plato said it best: "It does not matter if the cobblers and masons fail to do their jobs well, but if the guardians fail, the democracy will crumble."[2] (*Republic*).

2   Plato, *The Republic* (Penguin Classics, New Edition, 2007).

Many who serve in the law enforcement community have faced life-threatening scenarios. Over the course of my career, I drew my weapon on a number of occasions, thankfully never being required to pull the trigger. Over a twenty-eight-year career as a police officer, my brother fought for his life on numerous occasions. He's the "real cop" in the family. Every day across this great nation, law enforcement officers put their lives on the line to serve their community. It's a tremendous honor and responsibility. To quote a great George Strait song, "The Weight of the Badge," "It [the badge] doesn't weigh a lot. Until you put it on, then the weight of it is staggering."

Trust me: I know a guardian when I see one. On September 11, 2001, I had a front-row seat to witness guardians in action. They personified service and sacrifice. They are some of the finest, and their continued efforts allow this republic to survive.

That brings us to warriors. In the weeks and months following 9/11, our warriors went to work while the nation healed. Their "work" lasted more than twenty years in places like Afghanistan, Iraq, Libya, Syria, and others. One can have a spirited debate on the wisdom and validity of some of these conflicts. But on one issue, there is no debate. Since 9/11, the United States has not suffered from another terrorist attack of that magnitude (or close) on our home soil. Our citizens sleep soundly at night because our warriors "own the night," wreaking havoc on our enemies in all corners of the globe.

To use a quote attributed to George Orwell, "People sleep peaceably in their beds at night because rough men stand ready to do violence on their behalf." Simply put, the warriors protect the citizens by answering the bell overseas, bringing the fight to our enemies so that our enemies cannot bring the fight to us. I am forever grateful for these "rough men" and women who sacrifice so our republic and her people can prosper in peace.

Civilians, citizens, guardians, and warriors—if you feel the call to serve your community as a guardian or your nation as a warrior, go for it. You will never be wealthy, but you will always be fulfilled. You will live, and possibly even die, with a full heart because you are serving with like-minded brothers and sisters as you protect something greater than yourself. You will be part of the few who dedicate their minds and train their bodies to "quell the storm and ride the thunder." Most will not be called into such service, nor are they wired for it. But we can all *choose* to be citizens and not settle on being the self-absorbed bystander who is a civilian.

As we jump back into the story, let me be clear. On 9/11 in New York City, the citizens far outweighed the civilians. Evil, driven by hate, thought it would win the day. Nope. Citizens, driven by love, stood strong. The men and women who rallied with me in the lobby of that bank could have headed north to the safety of clean air and sunshine. But they chose to band together as citizens. Therefore, we headed south, as a unit, into the darkness. Into the unknown.

We made it back to the intersection of Church Street and Vesey Street, where we remarkably reconnected with Frank. What we discovered was staggering. Death ruled and reigned. Frank, Rob, John, and I could not believe our eyes. As we stood in amazement, we realized, other than ourselves, there was only one thing alive in the intersection of Church and Vesey streets.

Fire.

CHAPTER 10

BURNING RING OF FIRE

The art of war is simple enough. Find out where your enemy is. Get at him as soon as you can. Strike him hard as you can, as often as you can.
—Ulysses S. Grant

APPROXIMATELY 1130 HOURS, SEPTEMBER 11, 2001, CORNER OF CHURCH STREET AND VESEY STREET, NEW YORK CITY

Raging fire. We were back at the northwest corner of the World Trade Center site. A hallowed place now forever known as Ground Zero. The intersection of Church Street and Vesey Street would serve as our "battlefield" for the remainder of the day. It was time to get to work, but we were frozen. Frank, Rob, John, and I stood motionless as we took in the scene with awe.

Everything in sight, I mean everything, was on fire.

If you want to know what hell on earth looks like, allow me to describe. Heat was emanating from the street. The intersection was cluttered with civilian cars that had been abandoned. In addition, the intersection was packed with all sorts of emergency service vehicles: police cars, fire trucks, and FDNY ambulances. Almost all of them were burning. Some were crushed by debris and slowly burning underneath.

Others were already raging with flames. We witnessed gas tanks in cars begin to pop off under the weight of small controlled explosions.

To make matters worse, the entire scene was covered in paper. That's because over two hundred floors of office space lay before us in rubble. Therefore, office paper seemed to cover every square inch of the area, and it was fueling the burning ground all around us. John Beck would later say, "It looked like another planet."

We stood still as our brains processed the intersection and calculated what to do next. I wasn't motionless for long because my pants were on fire. I looked down to see the bottom of my pants leg beginning to burn. I quickly swatted down the tiny flames and soon realized I needed to be careful where I stepped. Needless to say, I could not totally avoid the fire with every step. At the end of the day, my pants were several inches shorter, and the soles of my shoes were warped and malformed from the constant heat.

At this point, we noticed a large NYPD Emergency Services Unit (ESU) truck in the intersection. Members of the NYPD ESU serve as kind of a "jack-of-all-trades" unit. They execute various roles that include but are not limited to SWAT (tactical elements), urban rescue, water rescue, and hostage negotiations. The ESU truck was beginning to catch fire from underneath. I figured it housed emergency equipment that might prove useful in our efforts as we prepared to get into the fight. For maybe the first time that day, I was correct.

I climbed to the top of the truck bed and began scouring its contents. John and Rob stood at the bottom as I threw random gear and equipment down to them. I can't remember everything we "acquired" from the NYPD vehicle, but I know we utilized flashlights, helmets, bright orange vests, and a pry bar. Underneath the truck, the fire began to expand, and one of my companions wisely advised me to jump down. We geared up as best we could, strapping on the helmets and vests in preparation to do the next thing. Rob inexplicably threw a scuba breathing apparatus on his back in an attempt to breathe clean air. He quickly realized it was folly and ditched the scuba gear.

Before we go any further, allow myself to make fun of . . . myself. It's important to understand the literal environment of our battlefield at the moment. Visibility was still awful as we couldn't see further than maybe half a block. In addition, random debris was falling from neighboring buildings. Despite the worst being over, it was still an active scene with dangers in all directions. Therefore, the helmets were important to protect our noggins from falling chunks of randomness. And the orange vests helped us keep track of each other in the hazy debris cloud. Smart use of borrowed gear, right?

OK, here's where it gets awkward. Both pieces of gear proved valuable in the hour or so to follow. But, eventually, the falling debris stopped, and the air surrounding the scene mostly cleared, drastically improving the visibility as the sunshine won over the debris cloud. Therefore, after an hour or so, Rob and John shed their gear and continued our efforts in plain clothes. That's because Rob and John were observant Special Agents. Apparently, I was not. I went on to wear the helmet and vest for hours, long after the air cleared and the debris falling debris ceased. I've included a photo of the three of us in which Rob and John look like normally dressed haggard humans fighting hard while I look like a helmeted clown in suit pants and a life jacket. This photo was used for years around my office to make fun of me in a kind-hearted way.

If you read too fast, you may have missed something in my narrative. I described the orange vest as a life jacket. To this day, John and Rob insist the vests were portable flotation devices (PFDs), commonly referred to as life jackets. I refuse to acknowledge their view. They were orange vests, plain and simple. Please do not take my self-deprecating humor in the wrong way. The entire day, especially this scene, was horrific. But in the law enforcement (and military) community, we often use humor to deal with the evil we encounter on a daily basis. It's an essential defense mechanism. I hope you can allow me some grace in this regard.

All kidding aside, we were only halfway through our fight. Surrounded by fire and destruction, I surveyed the scene. That's when He hit me. The Lord almost literally put me on my knees in the middle of the intersection. He said to me, "I am with you. I have not forsaken you." He spoke to me, but He didn't use words. Rather, He used a mangled mess. I looked toward the southeast corner and noticed something that staggered me. It was a completely destroyed FDNY fire truck.

Think back to earlier in my story when WTC 2 (the South Tower) began to collapse. I mentioned sprinting up the block to escape the kill zone, knowing escape was likely impossible. At that time, I noticed an FDNY fire truck to my right, and I briefly considered sliding under the truck to get shelter from the falling tower. As I mentioned earlier, I took a step in that direction and then pivoted back left and continued running north up the block. At that moment, I wasn't sure what compelled me to avoid sliding under the truck because it seemed like a good idea at the time. My thought was *The sky is falling. Get under something huge and heavy for shelter.* Still not the worst idea, considering the circumstance.

However, as I stood motionless in the intersection, I knew why I avoided the fire truck. Because it was flattened like a pancake beneath steel beams. The tires were turned out parallel to the ground. Anything under that truck was destroyed. Anyone under that truck was dead.

In disbelief, I zombie-walked around the corner, eastbound on Vesey Street. I was looking for a pickup truck and coffee cart, the same truck and cart I almost decided to slide under for protection during my sprint for life. I couldn't find it. Why? Because the entire section of road was covered in heavy debris. Again, anyone under that pickup and cart was dead.

As tears trickled down my face, I fully realized why my lifeless body wasn't under one of those vehicles. "The heart of a man plans his way but the Lord establishes his steps" (Proverbs 16:9). So true. Finding cover had made sense at the moment because the sky was literally falling all around me. So why not seek shelter under a large object for protection? Well, the Scriptures say the Lord's thoughts and ways are higher (better) than our thoughts and ways.

God had spared me.

Three Challenging Questions

When I reflect on the big picture of my survival story, I pose three questions to myself: one answer I already know, one I'm still living out, and one answer I will never understand. My first question is "How did I survive?" The answer is clear to me. God spared my life twice, in order to die another day. For some reason, He did not call me home.

The second question is "Why did I survive?" Brothers, I am living out my why right now. This book, its message, and my ministry are the valiant purpose that drives my life. A wise pastor once told me, "God does not waste suffering. He uses it for your good, for His glory." Over the years, God has made it clear to me that He was not done with me, meaning my mission was yet to be completed. It would be a waste of my personal suffering for me to live a safe life of moral navel-gazing while the world burned around me.

I was built for this time, for this place, in pursuit of a greater God-ordained purpose. The good news is so were you. Why did I survive? The answer for me is simple. I was destined to be a father of four boys that my wife and I would cultivate into godly men. I was also created to reach men by equipping them to seek their higher calling, courageously execute it, and make an impact for Jesus in their community. That's why I was spared.

Which leads us to the third question: "Why did so many others, almost three thousand, not survive?" As I stated in chapter 9, that answer, I will never fully know. It's a level of suffering we, as the created, can never understand on this side of heaven. But I am able to take solace in a promise laid out by the apostle Paul that I mentioned earlier: "For now we see in a mirror dimly, but then face to face. Now I know in part; then I shall know fully, even as I have been fully known" (1 Corinthians 13:12).

APPROXIMATELY 1135 HOURS, SEPTEMBER 11, 2001, CORNER OF CHURCH STREET AND VESEY STREET, NEW YORK CITY

I collected myself and shifted focus back to the task at hand, fire everywhere. Time to "do the next thing," but what the heck was the next thing?

"Lord, what now?" I remember speaking aloud. The situation was bleak. Fire ruled the intersection, and the professionals trained to fight it were all gone, lost forever but never forgotten. Until more firefighters could respond from other parts of the city, Frank, Rob, John, and I decided we were the next best option. We were gonna take back the intersection. It was time to rein in the fire.

We gazed across the intersection to the southwest side, and none of us could believe our eyes. There stood a completely intact, undamaged fire truck. We approached it with caution as if it were a mirage. It was an answer to my prayer. God is in the business of not only answering prayers but also providing a means for his faithful servants. He provided a functional fire truck and even more. What good is a tool or weapon if you don't know how to use it? That was my immediate thought at the time.

Rob spoke first, boldly saying, "We should hook up a hose to that fire truck and start putting out the fires." Honestly, my first reaction was not helpful. It was born from momentary defeat and helplessness. I thought, *That is stupid. How the hell are we gonna do that?*

Before I could verbally express my frustration, John chimed in, "Yeah, I bet I can figure it out. I used to be a volunteer firefighter back home."

To be honest, I was still not convinced, but I fell in behind them anyway as we approached the truck.

We opened a side box and began to unravel a hose. Rob and I took it and walked away with the head of the hose, looking for our first target. There we stood, facing a car fire, with a limp hose, and losing more confidence in our brothers with each passing second. I looked back only to see John and Frank randomly turning knobs and sliding levers. Meanwhile, my pants caught fire again, so I began kicking the flames out with one foot while standing on the burning leg.

It was at that moment, off balance, leaning on one leg with my pants on fire, that water exploded from the nozzle in my left hand. The force nearly knocked us over as water shot straight into the air. Who says Jesus doesn't have a sense of humor? And he is faithful to humble and sincere prayers, both big and small. My simple prayer just moments earlier was "Lord, what now?" He answered with a clear mission (fight fires), equipped us with tools (a functional fire truck), and provided knowledge (personal expertise) in deploying the tools. God is good.

John quickly joined Rob and me at the head of the hose while Frank manned the truck. And so began our day as amateur firefighters. "Amateur" is being very kind because initially we were pretty terrible at it. The hose was out of control, we weren't working with any coordination, and I was aiming the hose with no consistency.

Our first objective was a burning NYPD car, and it took us forever to gain the upper hand. But eventually, the remaining flames breathed their last, and we reveled in our first victory. We switched our order on the hose so the man in front wouldn't tire quickly, selected our next target, and began dousing another NYPD cruiser with water. We learned quickly to concentrate our stream on small areas, one at a time, at the base of the flames. Now we were stacking victories on top of each other.

In a moment of levity, we heard Frank shouting. Apparently, a tire on his own government car was starting to catch fire. According to John, Frank screamed, "Screw carpooling! That's my new car!" Frank sprinted across the intersection as we laid down water in his path. Frank fired up the engine and drove it a couple blocks north. But without question, Frank returned once again to the scene to get back into the fight. Meanwhile, Rob tirelessly manned the nozzle as we continued to work the problem at hand.

We were on a roll. Not to brag, but we were dominating the intersection. The fires were on the ropes. One vehicle after another drowned as we extinguished the intersection and began working further down the block.

Men, this scenario serves as the perfect illustration for our lives. Please don't miss what was happening here: four men, focused on an objective, working as a team, each feeding off the others' courage, strength, and knowledge. Four men winning. Not winning the day but winning our little fight, together. We weren't putting out all the fire across six square blocks. We were just dominating our area of responsibility.

Men, please hear me. This is the secret to the manly Christian life. Men of integrity, executing God's purpose, courageously fighting together, and driven by the love of Christ in compassion. That's called living in victory. And when the men of God are winning the day, Satan is losing.

CHAPTER 11

EVERYTHING HAS AN OPPOSITE

*"All my life," Dienekes began, "one question has
haunted me. What is the opposite of fear?"*
—Steven Pressfield, *Gates of Fire*

At this point in the story, you probably have one of two
thoughts regarding me and my Service brothers. One, these
guys are nuts. Get the heck out of there. Or two, these guys
are courageous heroes with no fear. Well, both assessments
miss the mark. So, let's hit pause on the narrative for a bit and
dig into a significant issue.

Courage. What is it? What fuels it? What is fear? What
is the role of fear in regard to courage? Ultimately leading to,
what compelled four men to risk their lives in a fiery hellscape
for people they did not know and property they did not own?

The answer is complicated. And as you might have guessed,
the answer for me is embedded in a life of following Jesus.

Fear and Courage Are Cousins

The quote opening this chapter is taken from a fantastic piece
of historical fiction, *Gates of Fire,* by Steven Pressfield. *Gates
of Fire* recounts the valiant last stand of King Leonidas and his

three hundred Spartan warriors at the narrow rocky mountain pass, Thermopylae. For six days in 480 BC, the mighty Spartans and their Greek allies slaughtered the oncoming hordes of Persians, led by King Xerxes, as they fought in the bottleneck known as the "hot gates."

Pressfield's fictional account of this historical event has been devoured by soldiers and leaders all over the world for its insight into courage, leadership, sacrifice, and the art of war. The novel is told from the perspective of Xeones, one of three Greek Thermopylae survivors and an apprentice to a Spartan officer, Dienekes. In Pressfield's account, Dienekes is a highly decorated combat veteran who has earned the respect and admiration of the younger Spartans in his command. One night early in the campaign, prior to arriving at Thermopylae, Dienekes and his men are sitting around a fire and discussing deep philosophical issues (like any good ancient Greek). The issue brought to the forefront is the concept of fear, especially fear as it relates to courage in combat.

Dienekes regales his inexperienced troops with stories of bravery and inspiring sacrifice in battle. He says he has witnessed countless Spartans, men of valor, slaughter their enemies against great odds. But he notes something significant. Dienekes reveals to his men that each act of valor was ultimately driven by fear. A fear of losing. A fear of dying. A fear of not living up to the Spartan code. A fear of family dishonor within the tribe. Dienekes is deeply troubled by this reality because he wants to believe that courage, real courage, is a noble virtue of greater esteem than fear. But in his experience, men of valor, men of courage at their very core, were ultimately driven by fear.

It is then, as Dienekes rises to his feet, that he leaves his men with the same very question that has troubled his very soul. "All my life, one question has haunted me. What is the opposite of fear?"

Fear is powerful. Fear is primal. Fear has fueled winners, driven heroes, and spawned cowards of men since the beginning of time. Fear is so prevalent in life that the Bible says "do not fear" or "do not be afraid" 366 times! That's once for every day of the year and a bonus on your birthday. Why does God's Word command us not to be afraid so often? I'm guessing because we need to hear it on repeat.

So, you can see, fear has the power to control our actions and dominate our minds. But everything has an opposite. Left versus right. Up versus down. Hot versus cold. Happy versus sad. There must be an opposing force just as powerful and primal as fear. What is the opposite of fear?

To reach the answer to our question, we must discuss the relationship between fear and courage. Every human life faces fear at times. There is no such thing as living a "fearless life." The greater issue is how much currency we allot fear in our lives. Fear can be a temporary feeling or emotion that is quickly overrun by something greater. Or fear can be the fuel of your very being and serve as the motor that drives your life. The former is natural; the latter is destructive.

The Power of Fear

Years ago, I was assigned to the protective advance team for a Secret Service protectee in Ethiopia. The air was hot and humid, as you would expect. We would be operating in the lowlands of Ethiopia, along the Omo River Valley. It was an area where hippos were king, even causing accidents as they strayed onto the runway at the local airport. We landed via commercial aircraft at the remote airfield without incident.

Interestingly, attached to the Ethiopian commercial airfield was a small United States Air Force drone base. I can share this because the existence of this base was public knowledge. You can even Google it. We met briefly with the command team at the base to deconflict any issues and make them aware of our presence in their area of operations. The medical officer of the base gave us a quick briefing on the environmental hazards in the region. Apparently, the greatest threat in the area was not a local militia or terror cell. Rather, it was the super venomous black mamba snake. In fact, a black mamba had been spotted the previous week by other Air Force personnel at our hotel. This just got serious. We were advised the only reliable antivenom in the area was stored in the small lab on the drone base. The officer advised if we were bitten by the black mamba, we would only have fifteen to twenty minutes to live.

So, naturally, I asked, "Hey, Doc, how long does it take to drive from our hotel back to the base?"

The officer deadpanned, "Oh, only about fifteen to twenty minutes."

Hello, fear.

We arrived at our single-story hotel in the countryside. It sat on a hill, towering over the area, and was surrounded by jungle on all sides. A sign in the lobby advised, "Stay out of the jungle. Lions." OK, duly noted.

We dispersed to our rooms, and upon entry, I immediately looked under the bed, in the bed, up in the rafters, in the bathtub, and all around the toilet. No mambas. I quickly showered and changed clothes, inadvertently leaving my black belt lying on the white sheets of my bed. Later, our team gathered at the hotel restaurant for dinner. After dark, we carefully walked back to our rooms. Everyone had their flash-lights deployed in all directions. We were on black mamba watch!

I reached my room, opened the door, and turned on the light. "Ahh-eee-ohh-hee!" I screamed. Or something like a scream. It's a noise I had never made, nor have I made sense. It's a noise I've never heard from a human mouth. But there was a black mamba on my bed! Or, upon a second glance, my black belt was on my bed. I almost had a heart attack because of fear. The black mamba had dominated my attention. Therefore, I was focused on the fear. Fear ruled and reigned in my heart for hours until, eventually, I saw the mambas everywhere. That may be a funny story but it serves as an illustration for life.

I believe many of us are tip-toeing through life, consumed by, driven, and focused on fear. Fear is destructive, and it is born from lies. What are you fearful of? If you are honest with yourself and really took time to reflect, what's your answer? The list may include fear of being alone, failing, making mistakes, disappointing others, fear of rejection. Men, spe-cifically, are oftentimes fearful of being fully known, causing financial ruin, being exposed as a fraud, or not "having what it takes."

Well-known author John Eldredge writes, "It's not a ques-tion—it's the question, the one every boy and man is longing to ask. Do I have what it takes?" Eldredge continues. "Most men live their lives haunted by the question, or crippled by the answer they've been given."[3]

When I reflect on big fears in my life, there are a few. They include the following: Do I have what it takes to be a good father? Will my family be financially ruined by our Colorado land purchase? Can I be successful as a speaker and author in the second stage of my career? All of these doubts I have wrestled with at different seasons in my life, but eventually, they grew into full-blown fear.

Fear is real, and it can be helpful, but only if it is temporary in nature. However, a life driven by fear, or rather, consumed by fear, can lead to unrepentant sin, paralysis, and timidity. Men, living in fear will render you reckless or feckless! Recklessness will lead you down a path of sin and possibly irrational risk-taking as you try to compensate for the fear boiling in your bones. Your wife, children, friends, and community will have to deal with the damage left in your wake.

Conversely, living in fear can also make you feckless, meaning ineffective, indifferent, and futile. You become a passive man numb to his responsibilities, and the list of victims includes those closest to you. A man who doesn't embrace his responsibilities as a husband and father is not fit to lead his family. Reckless or feckless—it's like the two heads of a sledgehammer. Both are incapable of building up or creating. Both destroy.

You can "fake it till you make it" for a while and maybe even have some worldly success. If so, your house is built on a foundation of sand. That "sand" is lies because fear is born

3   John Eldredge, *Wild at Heart: Discovering the Secret of a Man's Soul* (Thomas Nelson, 2001).

from lies. Eventually, the storms of life will come, and your house built on the sand will easily wash away.

Genuine Courage Is a Product of Faith

The better way is a heart of real courage. What is courage? I love this question because a quick internet query will provide hundreds of witty quotes. One of my favorites is from the famous US Army WWII general George Patton: "Courage is fear holding on a minute longer." There it is again, courage and fear bound together, just like in Dienekes's experience.

Here's my take. Genuine courage is the sum of strength, love, discipline, and humility. It's a product of faith in the promises of God that enables one to face the unknown, difficulties, danger, and pain despite temporary fear. Genuine courage does not fail at its testing point.

Did I experience fear on 9/11? You bet I did. Were there moments where my actions were driven by fear? Heck, yes. Let's change the question. Was I fearful that day? Was I full of fear? Absolutely not. And that's not because I'm some double-tough super alpha Secret Service agent. It's because my heart was filled with something greater, more powerful than fear. Something not rooted in myself, something I couldn't conjure up on my own.

Something eternal.

Courage is a product of faith in the promises of God. As a Christian, I believe the Bible is not necessarily a book of rules. Do this; don't do that. It's not a book about what to do; it's a book about what has already been done for you! The Bible is also a book of promises, and all God's promises are true.

How does this relate to fear and courage? As I mentioned

earlier, in the Bible, we are commanded no less than 366 times to not be afraid. But here's the kicker: oftentimes, God couples that command with a promise. I (God) will be with you!

Let's look at just a few examples of the promises of God found in the Bible. In Judges 6, God calls out Gideon to rid Israel of the mighty Midianites. When Gideon expresses his doubt and fear, God says to him, "But I will be with you, and you shall strike the Midianites as one man" (Judges 6:16). Eventually, Gideon faces 137,000 Midianites with a mere three hundred warriors. Ridiculous odds! But God delivers victory for Israel, and Gideon enters battle with zero fear in his heart. How do I know? Because, just before the battle begins, Gideon declares to his valiant three hundred, "Arise, for the Lord has given the host of Midian into your hand . . . Look at me and do likewise."

Did you catch that? On the cusp of battle, Gideon basically says, "Hey, y'all, watch this!" What follows? Victory. Where did his courage come from? His faith in the promise that the mighty God was with him.

The Bible is full of promises that God will never leave us. Sometimes, He calls us into great risks but always assures us of His never-ending presence. In Exodus 3, God commands Moses to outright challenge the most powerful man on the earth, Pharaoh. "But Moses said to God, 'Who am I that I should go to Pharaoh and bring the children of Israel out of Egypt?' He (God) said, 'But I will be with you'" (Exodus 3:11–12). Moses proceeds to confront Pharaoh with a fierce boldness that brings the powerful king to his knees. Victory.

In the book of Joshua, the Israelites were finally on the precipice of entering the Promised Land. But their ancestral home was full of powerful tribes. Fear was rampant throughout the Hebrew camp. But God emboldened their leader, Joshua, with two commands followed by a promise. "Have I not commanded you? Be strong and courageous. Do not be frightened, and do not be dismayed, for the Lord your God is with you wherever you go" (Joshua 1:9). Have courage. Fear not. I am with you. Joshua proceeds, and guess what follows? Victory.

We find courage in the Psalms because the Lord promises us, on repeat, that he is with us. "Even though I walk through the valley of the shadow of death, I will fear no evil, for you are with me; your rod and your staff, they comfort me" (Psalm 23:3–4).

"God is our refuge and strength, a very *present* [my emphasis] help in trouble. Therefore we will not fear though the earth gives way, though the mountains be moved into the heart of the sea, though the waters roar and foam, though the mountains tremble at its swelling . . . The nations rage, the kingdoms totter; he utters his voice, the earth melts. The Lord of hosts is with us; the God of Jacob is our fortress" (Psalm 46: 1–3, 6–7).

Feel the power of the prose. Though nations rage and kingdoms totter, I will not be fearful because God is with me and will never leave me. Victory. Our daily problems and big life decisions pale in comparison to the presence and power of our mighty God.

Our God, King Jesus, is a "with-you" God. He tells us on repeat that we should fear not because he is with us, will never leave us, and will never forsake us. That alone should give us tremendous courage.

No Matter What Happens, I Will Get to You

My family loves the great outdoors. One of our favorite things to do is raft the Arkansas River in Colorado. We don't pay a bunch of money for a guided tour in a huge, high-walled boat. You know, the "half-day" float trip that only takes about two hours. Instead, we have our own inflatable kayaks, and we paddle down the river ourselves. The kayaks, affectionately known as "rubber duckies," sit very low in the water, which greatly increases the fun and guarantees you get soaked. The river is always cold, but on one summer day, we needed to cool off. The breeze gave the air a chill, but the sun was bright, quickly warming our rubber rafts and life vests.

Taking a family of six down the river in three separate kayaks is a challenge, not to mention stressful. One of my sons, Nate, was not a fan of any water sport. He has since grown out of it, but at the time, he was fearful of our rafting adventures. On this particular day, just prior to launching, I could tell Nate was more nervous than usual. I pulled him aside and inquired.

He said, "I'm scared of the section with the big rock in the middle, you know, where mom and I flipped over last time." Ah yes! I had forgotten. On our last trip the previous summer, Nate and Heather hit a large rock sideways, and it immediately dumped them both over the side. They easily rode the rapids on their butts into calm water and managed to eddy out to the river bank. But Nate was shaken that day, and now the fear had returned.

I put my hand on his shoulder, looked young Nate dead in the eyes, and made a promise. "Nate, I am a United States Secret Service Rescue Swimmer. I am literally trained in white water rescue. More importantly, I am your father. No matter what happens out there, I will get to you. Trust me."

It worked. The lower lip ceased to quiver, and the gathering tears ceased to expand. Nate was assured that I was with him and capable of rescuing him.

We had a great day on the water until we approached that same darn rock in the middle of a tricky section of the river. We paddled along a lazy turn as we entered a new section of white water. We began bouncing up and down with delight as I led our little convoy out of the turn and into fast water. There it was, just staring at us. A large rock, about six feet wide and protruding four feet out of the water. You have to navigate this section just right. The current pulls you left, but at the last moment, it requires you to paddle hard to the right to avoid treacherous rocky shallows. If you don't get to the right soon enough, you might just hit that big rock. Daniel and I cleared it, Sam and Ben cleared it, and then, well, not so much.

Heather and Nate hit the rock sideways again, except this time they didn't flip. They were stuck.

Their kayak was hung up on the rock in a precarious position. The rest of us rode the rapids down to the calm water and paddled to the left bank. Sam, being the oldest, secured the kayaks and calmed his younger brothers. I grabbed the throw rope and began rock hopping up the river. My eyes succumbed to tunnel vision on Heather and Nate. With lungs burning and heart pounding, I slipped and sloshed my way toward my wife and son. The cold water numbed my feet, making the rock hopping more difficult.

After getting perpendicular to them, it was clear I could not reach them on foot. Nate was scared but composed, and

Heather was calm, nerves of steel. She's the tough one in the family. Heather was better positioned in the kayak. She knew she could fall backward into the river and the current would easily move her around the rock. I was worried if Nate did the same, he might get pinned against the rock. I threw the rope to Nate, and he grabbed it tight. Simultaneously, they both flopped into the river, and I began to pull Nate in with all my might, which turned out to be unnecessary as he managed to get to the bank fairly easily under his own power. All was well.

We regathered on the bank downriver and took a well-earned break. I put my arm around Nate and pulled him aside. "I promised I would get you, and I did. I am your father, and I will always do whatever it takes to protect you. But, Nate, imagine just how much more Jesus loves you. I will not always be with you. Jesus will. I will not always be strong enough. Jesus will. God is with you. Don't live life in fear. You are never alone. I love you, son."

He just needed to come face to face with the truth: Dad may not always be there, but Jesus is always with me, and that's all I need.

I was overcome with joy in Nate, considering how he handled the situation. In the face of fear, he was calm and steady (probably more so than me!). As a result of the trial, he was now stronger and more confident on the water. My heart was full of pride for my son. That day stands as my favorite moment in life, thus far, with Nate.

One of the keys to a life of genuine courage is to breathe deeply in the truth of God's promise that he is with you in all things at all times. When Jesus enters the world, the Gospel of Matthew declares He is to be called Emmanuel, meaning

"God with us" (Matthew 1:23). His Spirit, which we will discuss in chapter 13, is one that provides us power, strength, and self-control. The Spirit of God resides in the heart of every believer and, therefore, is always with us.

That Spirit is, among other things, that of the Lion of Judah. We, believers in Christ, are literally "lion-hearted." We just don't act like it. God is with us. Take heart. Have courage.

CHAPTER 12

COURAGE IS A CHOICE

A man without courage is a knife without an edge.
—Benjamin Franklin

Let's examine another component of genuine biblical courage often overlooked—humility. It's the secret ingredient, maybe even the secret weapon, to biblical courage. Humility is succinctly defined in the Bible as follows: "Do nothing from selfishness or empty conceit, but with humility of mind regard one another as more important than yourselves; do not merely look out for your personal interest, but also for the interest of others" (Philippians 2:3–4).

I believe this was my guiding principle for my actions on 9/11. This is what fueled my scandalous remark, "Let's go be heroes." That's the answer to our previous question: Why would a guy risk his life for those he does not know and for property he does not own? I see the hand of God (God's will) in all things. I live in the reality that I can't control all of my daily circumstances. For some reason, still largely unclear to me, God placed me at Ground Zero on 9/11. But He was with me, and He guided me. Of this, I have zero doubt.

I draw additional insight into humility from this passage of Scripture: ". . . clothe yourselves with humility toward one another, for God is opposed to the proud, but gives grace to the humble. Therefore, humble yourselves under the mighty hand of God, that he may exalt you at the proper time" (1 Peter 5:5–6). When we submit ourselves to the will of the Creator of the universe, He will use His creation as His instrument of compassion.

A truly humble man is so rightly related to his Creator that he is not affected in a negative way by daunting challenges or fear. He fears only the Lord, which allows him to humbly submit his thoughts and actions to Him. "Fear of the Lord is the beginning of wisdom" (Proverbs 9:10). Fear of the Lord can best be described as a state of jaw-dropping awe in the might and majesty of the Creator. Awe leads to submission of self and a humble heart. A humble heart is a courageous heart.

In my Secret Service career, I had the honor of training with and working alongside an elite group of valiant warriors. They are not glory hounds. They're quiet professionals. They are the humblest collection of operators I have ever witnessed. They are not combat oriented. They do not train to kill; they train to rescue. They are the men and women who make up the United States Coast Guard Rescue Swimmers.

Being a USSS Rescue Swimmer myself, I in no way compare myself to them. Think of it this way. If they are the Major Leagues, then we are the High School JV team. This is a collection of superfit, highly trained, badass professionals who willingly enter the roughest seas "so that others may live." Yet each one of them will admit to a humbling reality.

Regardless of their ability or training, they are no match for the power of moving water. Fast-moving, powerful water will throw you wherever it wants you to go. Their humility is spawned from their awe and respect for the power of moving water. Such is the humble man in awe of his Creator.

Humbled by the River

I have another personal story to serve as an illustration regarding humility. It happened on the Arkansas River. Yep, the same river. Yep, the same section and that same darned rock! A couple years after our scary incident with Nate, we found ourselves in a similar circumstance. It was a beautiful day in south-central Colorado. Tourists flocked into town, many even dipping their toes in the cold river. The skies were clear, and the winds were calm. But the river, well, that was different.

It was earlier in the season than when we normally visited; therefore, the spring snowmelt created large runoff in the river. The water was huge, much faster than usual.

Sam, my oldest son, leaned forward and whispered, "Maybe we shouldn't go out today. That river looks rough."

"Nah, we got this. It's gonna be a blast!" was my less-than-humble response. We got underway, quickly zipping down the river. Before we knew it, at about the seventh mile, we approached our not-so-favorite section of the river. Well, this time, I crashed into the rock. I never even saw it. We were rolling so fast. With the water moving at a ferocious pace, we didn't stand a chance. Immediately, we were flipped over, plunging into the cold Arkansas. To make matters worse, we were rolling three deep in the kayak that day. I had with me my two youngest sons, Ben, twelve, and Daniel, ten, at the time.

It didn't go well.

Anyone with white water training knows if you fall overboard while in the rapids, simply roll on your back and float with your butt up and feet pointing downstream. You will likely avoid hitting your butt on large rocks, and your feet will not get caught in any debris or crevices. The worst thing you can do is put your feet down and fight the current because you can easily get your foot trapped, and the current will push you under. Game over.

Well, I have to admit I panicked. Ben and Daniel were thrown to the right of the rock while I was shoved to the left.

We were separated, and it freaked me out.

They were my responsibility. *Jesus help me*, I said to myself. I had one hand on the inverted kayak and began swimming across the rapids to reach them. I wasn't making any progress. Then I put my feet down to push off the rocks for assistance, exactly what I shouldn't have done. My legs were getting blasted as my shins slammed into one rock after another. Excruciating pain ran up my back.

Meanwhile, Ben was riding the rapids on his back with his feet downstream, just as I had trained him. Young Daniel, however, was on his stomach facing me, screaming for help. Terror in his eyes, my heart was broken. I couldn't make it to him. My strength was no match for the powerful rapids.

I yelled at him to roll over, and he did. I was trying to keep the kayak in my possession so we wouldn't be stranded on the river. But it was inverted, making it almost impossible to make progress across the rapids. But my decision was an easy one. I had to let go of the kayak and make it to Daniel.

Then, just as I was about to release the kayak from my grasp, I heard his brother yell, "Daniel, I got you!" I looked up to see Ben return for his younger brother. Ben grabbed Daniel's vest and, as they entered the calm water, began dragging him to the bank. They had to get to the bank before the next set of rapids. Together, they powered themselves to the sand as I struggled to drag the inverted kayak to the bank.

I collapsed to my knees, out of breath, and pulled my boys close to me in a side hug. My legs seemed destroyed. I was sure I had broken a shin. But in a matter of minutes, I was able to stand, and the pain began to subside. No broken bones.

I put my hand on Ben's shoulder. "I'm proud of you, son. You were fearless and selfless. I couldn't have done that without you."

Ben, always confident, responded with a crooked smile. "I got you, Dad." Ben had made a choice. Courage is a choice. He chose to put his safety aside for the betterment of his younger brother. He chose to slow his descent down river, swim toward his brother in the calmer water, and grab Daniel by the collar. Together, they kicked and pulled themselves to shore. Ben chose to look out for not only his own interests but also those of others. He literally chose to obey Philippians 2:3–4.

I was a proud father. I slapped Ben on the back and grinned, then shouted one of our family jokes. "One step closer to manhood, son!"

However, my manhood was shaken. I had failed. I was humbled.

That night over dinner, I cried as I confessed my arrogance to the family, and I asked their forgiveness. We should have never been on the river that day. The water was too big and fast, creating an environment beyond our collective skill level.

By the way, Sam (paddling solo) and Heather and Nate (together) managed the rapids perfectly that day, no issues. In retrospect, as the most experienced person in our group, managing three separate kayaks in those conditions was too much to ask of myself. In my panic, I had committed the cardinal sin of dropping my feet in the rapids. Only by the grace of God had my foot not gotten trapped. I was humbled. I was physically fit, knowledgeable of the river, and trained in white water rescue. Yet still, I failed. I was bailed out by a courageous twelve-year-old.

I learned a valuable life lesson that day on the violent Arkansas River. I picture the river as a metaphor for life. It's full of twists and turns, joys and sorrows. The river and life both pose obstacles (rapids) to conquer and easy seasons of relative comfort (slow, still water). They're both terrifying, fun, and exhausting, often in that order. And sometimes, the river (and life) will suddenly dump you upside down. The lesson I learned is simple. Through all that life has to offer, I will not live in fear but rather focus on the promises of God.

He is with me and for me. He has a plan for me. And that plan will be used for good because I am called according to His purpose (Romans 8:28). His will is my purpose. I can have confidence in humbly submitting to His path. As His created being, I will not go against the will of my Creator. It's just as futile as swimming against the mighty rapids. I will submit my life under the mighty hand of God, and He, not me, will do great things. A faithful heart is a courageous heart. A humble heart is a courageous heart.

Choose to Chance the Rapids

I'll offer one further insight as a preview to the last few chapters of this book. There is danger on the river (and life); there is joy on the river (and life). Success and failure await you on the river. It may feel "safe" to sit on the banks, maybe occasionally dipping a toe in the rippling edges. But a deep dive into the river is where we are called to be.

God didn't create the river, life, to be watched from afar. He has a place for you there, a role for you. Will you have the courage to dive in and ride the waves? Will you leave the dry comfort of the shoreline, or will you instead dare to swim headlong into the mighty rapids of life?

Let's close with our Greek friends from Pressfield's *Gates of Fire*. After Dienekes leaves his men around the fire, he's still wrestling with his question. What is the opposite of fear? He turns to his colleague Alexandros and says, "How does one conquer fear of death, that most primordial of terrors, which resides in our very blood, as in all life, beasts as well as men? Dogs in a pack find courage to take on a lion. Each hound knows his place. He fears the dog ranked above and feeds off the fear of the dog below. This is how we Spartans do it, counterpoising to fear of death a greater fear: that of dishonor. Of exclusion from the pack. But is that courage? Is not acting out of fear of dishonor still, in essence, acting out of fear?"

Alexandros asked what he was seeking.

Dienekes replied. "Something nobler. A higher form of mystery. Pure. Infallible."

CHAPTER 13

THE OPPOSITE OF FEAR IS LOVE

*"Do you remember the night, Xeo, when we sat with
Ariston and Alexandros and spoke of fear and its
opposite?" I said I did. "I have the answer to my question
. . . The opposite of fear," Dienekes said, "is love."*
—Steven Pressfield, *Gates of Fire*

There it is, laid out before us in all its simplicity. The answer to our big question. The opposite of fear is love.

In *Gates of Fire*, our hero Dienekes came to this conclusion after reflecting on his final days in battle versus the relentless Persians. It was the night he would lead a Spartan strike team into the enemy camp. The objective of the raid was to assassinate the Persian King, Xerxes. It was, for all intents and purposes, a one-way trip. A suicide mission. As the team gathered around the campfire, they made their final preparations for the raid. Like every warrior does, they spoke of their fallen brothers and the realities of impending death.

At this point, the lowly regarded man named Suicide (not joking), says the following: "When a warrior fights not for himself, but for his brothers, when his most passionately sought goal is neither glory nor his own life's preservation, but to spend his substance for them, not to prove unworthy of them ... then his heart truly has achieved contempt for death, and with that he transcends himself and his actions touch the sublime." It is then that Dienekes utters his decree—the opposite of fear is love.

Let's round out the remainder of our definition of genuine courage. I defined courage earlier as the sum of strength, love, discipline, and humility. It's a product of faith in the promises of God that enables one to face the unknown, difficulties, danger, and pain despite temporary fear.

In chapter 11, we examined the promises of God, revolving around the truth that he is a "with-you" God. Chapter 12 tackled humility as the secret ingredient to courage. Now, let's fully unpack one last principle. In the heart of a believer, love knocks out fear every time.

Love Is Undefeated

Fear is powerful. Fear is primal. Fear drives a man to great heights or perilous depths or both. But one thing is more powerful: love. Hidden inside the brilliance of Pressfield's fiction is an eternal truth. From the Christian perspective, God is love. In the presence of God's love, fear cannot exist.

As I mentioned in the opening of this book, I'm just a guy. I don't have a bunch of letters before or after my name to denote my advanced degrees. I'm no theologian or pastor. But I can offer you three simple Scriptures that, when properly applied, enable a man to live in love, not fear. If you are a practicing Christian, purposefully living out God's will in your life, then the love of Christ is your driving force, not fear.

If you are a Christian who is consumed by fear, then may I suggest you are not being obedient to the will of God.

My prayer is this chapter will give you hope for a nearly fearless future. I want these three truths (promises) to sink into your bones in the hope that you can see at least a fraction of how much God loves you. Consider each of these passages as an arrow striking deep into the heart of fear in your life.

ARROW 1

There is no fear in love; but perfect love casts out fear, because fear involves punishment, and the one who fears is not perfected in love. We love, because he first loved us.
—1 John 4:18–19

This is an extremely rich passage. But remember: I'm just a guy. I'm gonna keep this real neat and simple. The perfect love of Jesus casts out all fear as if it were a bright flashlight piercing through a dark room. Just as darkness cannot exist in the presence of light, deep fear cannot exist in the presence of God's perfect love.

So what does that mean for us? Let's be real. Many Christians wrestle with this lie: "God can't fully love me because I mess up (sin) all the time." Nonbelievers who are contending with the Bible and the notion of saving faith wrestle with the very same lie. Both speak this lie into their souls: "I'm not good enough."

And guess what. On your own, that is absolutely correct. However, as we discussed in chapter 6, Jesus redeemed our past, present, and future sins by sacrificing himself on the cross.

Because of that reality, a Christian can walk with confidence, knowing he or she is cleansed from all sin (1 John 1:5–7).

Now catch this; take a look at Arrow 1. Therefore, there is no punishment from sin because we are perfected in his love. The apostle Paul takes this radical love a step further when he declares; "Therefore, there is no condemnation for those who are in Christ Jesus" (Romans 8:1). The Greek word in that text for *condemnation* was a judicial term typically used in that time to declare someone "not guilty."

Please don't miss the significance of this declaration. Romans 8:1 states for Christians that not only is there no eternal punishment for sin, but we are actually declared not guilty, as if we never committed the sin, only because of Jesus. As a Christian who still wrestles with sin, this blows my mind.

Years ago, when my son Ben was a toddler, he once got kicked out of Sunday school class for misbehaving. I was notified to pick him up from his classroom, and he sat with Heather and me for the remainder of the church service. He was quietly sitting beside me as he wrestled with guilt and embarrassment, slowly wiping away tears. Full of shame, he gently slipped onto my lap.

Several minutes later, the Spirit of God compelled me to speak. I leaned into his left ear and whispered, "You're my boy. I love you." His reaction was instant. His tension released; he tucked his head into my neck and embraced the grace from his father. My words released him from his guilt and shame. Despite his poor choices (sin), he was still my boy, and I still loved him.

Now, apply this illustration to Romans 8:1 and magnify the love by a trillion. God not only declares we are still his children but also declares us not guilty through the blood of Christ from the sin. It's simply hard to comprehend.

Now hear me clearly. We may be forgiven of our sins, but there are still consequences for sin. Therefore, we must wage war against it. Sin hardens our hearts toward the things of God. In no way should we just sin more so God's grace can abound more (Romans 6:1–2). In the words of Jim Denison, "Sin always takes you further than you wanted to go, keeps you longer than you wanted to stay, and costs you more than we wanted to pay."[4]

Consider the promise of Arrow 1 (1 John 4:18–19) and walk in the truth. And then, for a moment, you will catch a glimpse of how much God loves you. Armed with a promise such as this, we can lay aside our shame and embrace the grace lavished upon us. Perfect love is greater than fear.

A Spirit of Power

ARROW 2

For God has not given us a spirit of timidity, but of power and love and self-control.
—2 Timothy 1:7

The apostle Paul is very clear in this passage that we, as children of God, do not possess a fearful spirit in our souls. The spirit that resides in the heart of all believers is one of love and, therefore, power. Timidity in modern language is defined as the state of lacking in self-assurance, courage, or bravery. In the context of this passage, the Greek word for

---

4   Jim Denison, "Can I Really Overcome Temptation and Sin?" (The Denison Forum, March 23, 2019).

timidity denoted "shameful fear," typically rooted in "selfish character." Therefore, as the Lion of Judah lives in our hearts, love overcomes our "shameful fear." This enables the believer to be bold in deeds and actions.

Pressfield's Spartans, with warriors' hearts, also touch on this truth: "When a warrior fights not for himself, but for his brothers, when his most passionately sought goal is neither glory nor his own life's preservation, but to spend his substance for them . . . then his heart truly has achieved contempt for death."

The Bible makes the case even more clear in the words of Jesus found in John 15:12–13: "This is my commandment, that you love one another just as I have loved you. *Greater love has no one than this, that one lay down his life for his friends*" [my emphasis]. Do you see the humility found in this passage? We can love our brothers so much that we willfully spend our very "substance" for them.

This same spirit was guiding my actions throughout all my ordeals on 9/11. It wasn't some kind of John Wayne macho courage that I was able to muster together. I was only able to execute what I did because the spirit of Jesus was the driving force behind my actions. And that spirit is not one of fear but one of love and power. Our Arrow verse also mentions having discipline or self-control, again, not coming from us but rather the Spirit of Jesus in our hearts.

Think about how you experience life when it's driven by fear. There's a constant state of frenzied chaos, doubt, and lack of confidence. The Spirit of God described in 2 Timothy 1:7 brings order and structure as we are empowered to be steadfast and immovable in the works of the Lord. This same

Spirit instructs us to deny worldly desires and to live sensible and righteous lives (Titus 2:12).

Here's the bottom line. While we may suffer from temporal moments of fear and doubt, with Christ in our hearts, we can move with confidence through the fear and into God's love and power. Ultimately allowing our thoughts and actions to be driven by love, not fear.

An Adopted Son of the King

ARROW 3

For all who are led by the Spirit of God, these are the sons of God. For you have not received a spirit of slavery leading to fear again, but you have received a spirit of adoption as sons by which we cry out, "Abba! Father!"
—Romans 8:14–15

You are not a slave. You are a son of the King. *Bam!* Allow that reality to punch you in the face. Let's keep this really simple. When someone accepts Christ as their Savior, they receive a new heart, becoming a new creation with the Spirit of God residing in their heart (2 Corinthians 5:17; 1 Corinthians 3:16). That Spirit, as mentioned earlier, is not one of fear but rather one of power, love, and self-control. Our passage above, Arrow 3, states that we are no longer slaves to sin living in fear of punishment.

Romans 8:2 says, "For the law of the Spirit of life has set you free in Christ Jesus from the law of sin and death." This verse, coupled with Arrow 3, makes it clear we are no longer fearful slaves (to sin), yet instead, we are adopted sons of the

King. Think about that for a second. Let it sink in. King Jesus, the Alpha and Omega, the Creator of the universe, calls you his son (or daughter).

Consider the differences between the way a slave is treated and the way a son is treated. We deserve to be treated as slaves, yet we swim in the grace of Jesus, drinking deeply from the water of life.

This passage also speaks to the personal nature of our relationship with Jesus. The Scripture says we cry out to him, calling him "Abba, Father." "Abba" was an informal Aramaic term for father that conveyed a deep sense of intimacy. In modern terms, we can think of it as "Papa" or "Daddy." That's right, the Prince of Peace, the Lion of Judah, loves us so much that we possess the level of intimacy to call him "Papa."

Now, that may make you feel uncomfortable, but that doesn't make it untrue. I'm not sure how you feel about this truth. But if I can comprehend the magnitude of this sort of intimate love, I'm empowered to live with boldness of action, free from fear.

Several years ago, I sat in a lawn chair in my backyard, talking a man off the ledge. My friend Steve was in dire straits. His marriage was falling apart, and his career was in shambles, all due to his personal sin. Steve was a follower of Jesus, but the Enemy had grabbed hold of him and had taken a wrecking ball to his life. Steve was like a boxer, stuck in the corner, taking one body blow after another. The knockout punch was coming. He needed to get out of the corner.

Steve's crisis of identity came to a head while fishing with his young son. His boy slipped off the dock into the water. Steve reached down and grabbed his son's hand. He pulled with all his might, but he couldn't get his boy over the top. Steve began to panic. Suddenly, another man jumped into the water, lifted his son out up, and Steve pulled him in. His son was safe, but Steve was broken.

Embarrassed and full of shame, with tears in his eyes, he said to me, "I couldn't even save my own son." In his own mind, Steve was a loser, a failure, a man past the point of rescue. He was believing lies, so it was time to bring the truth.

I looked Steve dead in the eye and said forcefully, "Steve, you are not a loser. You're a son of the King!"

His reaction was instant. I saw life in his eyes, new life. It's as if he slipped the last punch, stepped right, and escaped the corner. It was the start of a new beginning. Now he was dancing on his toes with the new wind of truth in his sails. Steve kept fighting. Steve answered the bell again and again. Eventually, over time, Steve rebuilt his marriage and salvaged his career. But it all started with him denouncing one lie and believing the truth. He was a son of the King.

There are many ways in which you can implement these truths into your life. I'll quickly touch on two ways to apply. First, fear is not of God. Fear is of the Enemy. Therefore, when you are overcome with fear, take a pause and carefully examine the lies you may be believing. In the words of Jesus: "He (Satan) was a murderer from the beginning, and does not stand in the truth, because there is no truth in him. When he lies he speaks out of his own character, for he is a liar and the father of lies" (John 8:44).

The Father of Lies comes only to steal, kill, and destroy (John 10:10). Fear is born from lies, and the truth is born from God's faithful, loving promises. So, pause and take inventory of the lie you have inserted into your life and swap it out with truth. The truth can always be found in the Scriptures. Also, ask other wise and godly people in your life to reveal the lies you may be believing.

Second, literally, speak the truth of Scripture into your heart. Trust me: it works. This cannot happen unless you take the time to memorize certain passages as you read the Bible. Believe me: memorizing Scripture does not come easy for me, and that may be the case for you too. However, with a little effort over time, you can arm yourself with little arrows of truth to combat the lies used by the Enemy. For starters, try memorizing the three Arrows we discussed in this chapter. Then, find and memorize other passages that speak to you so you may be fully equipped.

Of Whom Shall I Be Afraid?

Let me give you a real-world example. Years ago, I was in Ethiopia, on the same protective mission I mentioned in chapter 11. Our protectee was touring with friends through many of the tribes of the Omo River Valley in Southern Ethiopia. Basically, each day, we jumped from village to village via a small fleet of helicopters. Each village was isolated and had its own customs and cultures. Toward the end of the trip, the tour guide suggested the party visit the reclusive Mursi tribe, typically found in the highlands. The Mursi were known for being standoffish to Westerners and even overly aggressive at times. To make matters more challenging, the Mursi are nomadic, never staying in one place very long. The decision was made to recon the highlands, locate the Mursi, and meet with them to ascertain their willingness to host a party of Westerners.

Well, guess who was tasked with this assignment? Yep, another agent named Peter and I prepared to take off with the guide to find the Mursi. At first, it was awesome. The air was thick and heavy as a blanket of humidity settled in with the rising of the sun. I was already sweating before 0800 hours. Peter and I, along with the pilot and guide, briefed over the details of the mission. Once complete, we sat in the sauna-like helicopter while the pilot spun up the engines. Time to get going.

Once in the air, I was excited to tackle the unknown. The pilot, formerly British special forces, was flying low and fast along the Omo River. Blaring through our headsets was Otis Redding's "Sittin' on the Dock of the Bay." It was nothing but good vibes. My head was bopping as I leaned into each turn of the chopper. It felt like I was in a movie. Then we hit the highlands, and something odd began to happen.

Fear began to creep into my heart.

The guide had briefed us that the Mursi are a mercurial bunch and highly unpredictable toward Westerners. He even told us most of the men would be armed with AK-47s, but "don't worry—ammunition is scarce." Great, what could go wrong? But here's the truth. The closer we got to locating the Mursi, the more fear entered my heart. The guide yelled in excitement as he saw a Mursi village nestled on a plateau. The pilot began to circle the area, looking for a safe place to land the helo. In my heart, and now in my mind, fear was beginning to win the battle. Within minutes, I found myself focused on the fear and not my mission.

Mission first! I inwardly screamed to myself. And then the Spirit of God compelled me to speak truth to the lies. He brought a verse to my mind I had memorized long before. One single verse. Silently, I began to speak the verse over and over again into my heart: *"The Lord is my light and my salvation; whom shall I fear? The Lord is the stronghold of my life; of whom shall I be afraid?"* (Psalm 27:1).

One single verse, on repeat in my mind, deeply penetrating my heart. I bet I said the verse thirty times before we touched down on that rugged plateau. The pilot killed the engine. I looked at Peter and gave him a nod.

"Let's do this," I said. I slid the door open and stepped onto potentially dangerous ground. I can honestly say, as my foot hit the ground, I had zero fear in my heart. Mursi men cautiously approached our party, half of which were armed with AKs. It didn't matter to me. I was bold. I was confident. I was fearless. Because I knew "the Lord is the stronghold of my life." I didn't talk myself into courage. I didn't muster together bravery from some inspirational speech. I simply spoke the living Word of God into my soul, and His perfect love cast out all my fear. Trust me, brothers: it works.

If God Is for Us, Who Can Be Against Us?

Let us review. God's perfect love casts out fear, and we don't live in fear of punishment because Jesus has paid the price for our sins. Because of this faith, the Spirit of God dwells within us, and that Spirit is not one of fear but rather of power, love, and self-control. Because we are a new creation, we are no longer "children of wrath." Rather, we are adopted sons of the King.

If you are a believer in Christ, then rest in this truth and allow it to power you through all of life with genuine courage.

If you are not a follower of Jesus, then let me ask you a question. Doesn't this sound freaking awesome? Who wouldn't want to be loved in such a manner and empowered by a never-failing Spirit?

It's there for you too. Just grab it. Wrap all of these promises, or arrows, together and put them in a quiver. Here's your quiver. It's a question and answer from the apostle Paul, Romans 8:31: "What then shall we say to these things? If God is for us, who can be against us?"

If all of these things are true, and they are, then what should we be afraid of? Who could possibly oppose the loving God that is with you and for you? It's all about perspective. On what do you choose to focus? The uncertainty, the daunting challenge, the potential pain? Or will you lock in on the truth, the power of his promises, and a love that can move mountains?

I once heard Pastor Tony Evans give a tremendous sermon on David and Goliath. Toward the end, Pastor Evans made a brilliant observation. Evans concluded his message with this thought that I will paraphrase here: "The Israelites saw a giant so big he couldn't be beat. David saw a giant so big he couldn't miss."

It's all about perspective. Will you focus on the lies or find courage in the truth? He is a "with-you" God. He has called you His own, He has a purpose for you, and He loves you far beyond what you can possibly fathom. Love is not just the opposite of fear. God's love is far greater than fear. Take heart. Have courage.

Darin Kinder deploying from a US Coast Guard MH-60 Jayhawk during a joint training exercise.

Darin Kinder on a protection assignment at JFK International Airport.

A damaged FDNY fire truck near the intersection of Church and Vesey streets. There is no way to be certain, but this truck could possibly be the one utilized by Darin and his colleagues. Source: Unknown.

Secret Service agents Rob Donovan (right), Darin Kinder (center wearing a helmet) and John Beck (left) fighting fires near the intersection of Church and Vesey Streets. The fourth individual is unknown.

Former USSS agent Tom Armas carrying an injured woman on 9/11/01. Tom would later leave the Secret Service and rejoin the United States Marine Corps. At the time of this writing, Armas had risen to the rank of Brigadier General. Source: Getty Images.

President George W. Bush moments after his famous "bullhorn speech".
Darin Kinder can be seen wearing a white hard hat, over the right shoulder of
NY Governor George Pataki. Source: Getty Images.

On September 14, 2001, Secret Service supervisor Frank Larkin (left) briefs
President Bush and other officials visiting the Ground Zero site.
Source: The White House.

PART III

NO CLEAN SUITS

CHAPTER 14

DO THE NEXT THING

*A good plan, violently executed now, is better than a
perfect plan next week.*
—US Army General George Patton

APPROXIMATELY 1230 HOURS, SEPTEMBER 11, 2001, CORNER OF CHURCH STREET AND VESEY STREET, NEW YORK CITY

We were winning. Frank, Rob, John, and I were taking back
control of the fiery intersection, one vehicle at a time. The gray
haze in the air was slowly beginning to dissipate. The bright
sun, now high in the sky, was piercing its way through the
gloom. Therefore, we were dripping in sweat. Unfortunately,
each minor victory (extinguished car fire) added to the haze
as dark smoke billowed from each smoldering vehicle. All
told, we probably extinguished six to eight vehicle fires. We
didn't have a grand plan to be executed in great detail. Just a
mission: dominate the intersection, now. Win "the next thing."

As time progressed, more FDNY personnel arrived on the
scene from other parts of the city. Soon we were surrounded
by real firefighters as they joined the fight. One might think,
The professionals are here. Let's back off. But honestly, the
thought never entered our minds. We were engaged with the
enemy, and we were going to finish it.

I do remember finding something a little strange about the scene. The firefighters overwhelmed the area and got to work. They brought in huge trucks and also began connecting lines to the fire hydrants on the street. Their hoses were much larger and more powerful than ours, and our lines quickly began to become tangled in the debris. Here's what I remember as strange: at no point in time did a single one of them tell us to stop or move out of the area. It appeared, at least temporarily, that we were one of them. This was an all-hands-on-deck circumstance. We were amateurs, but our acceptance on the scene emboldened our efforts. We just assumed we were doing something right and continued to proceed.

A half hour passed as the intersection became a hornet's nest of activity. I was in awe as I watched the professionals get to work. They were calm, efficient, and in relentless pursuit. What were they pursuing? An access point into the site to rescue their brothers and sisters in the rubble. Essentially, we were all making the scene safe so that rescue operations could begin.

Unfortunately for the amateur squad, we were at the end of our rope—literally. We were running out of hose length. I worked to untangle the hose from the rubble for more length as Rob and John continued to pour it on. Eventually, our line could reach no farther. We dropped our hose and assessed the scene.

We were in the middle of Vesey Street on the south side. I looked further west in despair. I was crushed. It was never a stated goal, but today, I can recognize our unspoken objective was to reach WTC 7. WTC 7 was our office building, our home away from home. But it was out of reach.

Luckily, the professionals were working their way down Vesey Street, relentlessly dousing fire as they progressed. I watched in hopeful anticipation as the FDNY liberated the block yard by yard. Then, suddenly, I witnessed firefighters make a hasty retreat back toward our direction. Apparently, the vanguard of the column realized WTC 5 was unstable and WTC 7 was burning furiously, creating a high-risk environment. The firefighting team was almost literally surrounded by unstable buildings, just waiting to collapse. They were ordered to pull back toward the intersection of Church Street and Vesey Street.

I can only assume the risk outweighed the reward; they had already lost too many brave men and women that day. I'm not sure who he was, but Rob and I were within earshot when we heard an FDNY on-scene commander speak into his radio something to the effect of "Number 7 is just gonna have to burn. We can't get to it."

My chin dropped to my chest as I took in a deep breath. Dominating my mind was one question: *Did all my guys get out in time?*

The imminent loss of WTC 7 was like taking a punch to the sternum, the wind knocked from my lungs. The four of us stood, almost motionless, in the center of the intersection. Rescue operations continued around us, but I suddenly felt useless. It's a sickening feeling I call "purpose lost." We were a unit that had been answering the bell all day, and now we lacked an objective. Frank was the only one of us with a Secret Service radio. It was no coincidence. The three very junior agents had neglected to grab any useful equipment during our hasty evacuation. Frank, being a veteran agent, grabbed our only useful form of communication.

While we took a pause in our action, I could hear Frank's radio clearly. Members of our New York Field Office had established a mobile command post nearby. We were gleaning small bits of information from the ongoing radio traffic. Sadly, the command post agent was repeatedly calling out for John and Tom (the agents I was previously with in Tower 1). There was no response. My heart sank as I considered the worst. Maybe Tom and John never made it out?

We stood listlessly in a daze for about twenty minutes. Perhaps we were crashing after yet another adrenaline dump. Suddenly, a cry pierced through the smoke, "We need man-power over here!"

Time to do the next thing.

The four of us ran in the direction of the shout toward WTC 5. We approached a side entrance of WTC 5 just in time to see several FDNY firefighters dragging two badly injured victims from the wreckage. One of the victims appeared to be dead, but the other was alive, although half of his face had been ripped from his skull. I had no idea how to treat such a wound, but Frank immediately took command of the situation. Prior to his Secret Service career, his Navy SEAL training included combat medicine, and he also served as a flight paramedic with the Maryland State Police. This guy was a one-man task force. He was more than qualified.

Frank stabilized the victim while someone comman-deered an abandoned ambulance that was in the intersection. The truck was in rough shape. Even its windows were blown out. But the engine fired up without hesitation. We lifted the victims into the truck, and to my surprise, Frank jumped in the back, barking orders to the firefighters in assistance. The doors slammed shut, and the truck accelerated, kicking up dust as I watched Frank leave the scene.

Rob, John, and I turned our attention to the entrance of WTC 5. We joined a group of about ten FDNY firefighters preparing to enter the building. It was determined there might be more survivors in the sublevels. We divided into groups of two or three and began the descent into the basement of WTC 5. Well, I thought it was the basement. We walked into a clearing, and I quickly realized we were in the mezzanine level of the WTC complex, which was basically an underground shopping mall.

Each group dispersed in different directions, armed only with flashlights and pry bars. The scene was eerie, to say the least. It resembled a set from a horror movie or some futuristic apocalyptic hellscape. The space was much quieter than the scene on the street. Oddly, we spoke in hushed tones as we searched the area foot by foot. The place smelled of damp pulverized concrete. The entire space was pitch black, with shattered glass on the ground and random support beams dangling from above. Just imagine standing in utter darkness, surrounded by brokenness.

But we went to work.

I carefully picked my path to avoid debris as I called out into the darkness, then optimistically waited in silence for a reply. A response that never came. We couldn't find any survivors. We continued on into the darkness for about fifteen minutes before we encountered another group of FDNY firefighters. They had come up empty as well. We were discussing our next move when a low rumble thundered in the near distance.

Almost immediately, the FDNY's radio crackled with a command. WTC 5 was in danger of collapsing. Evacuate forthwith! To say we "turned and burned" is an understatement. We hustled through the dark maze, desperate to find our exit. I tripped over debris and fell to the ground. Picking glass from my hands, I sprinted to the stairwell.

I emerged from the stairwell and was nearly blinded by the daylight. After catching our breath, John, Rob, and I stood on the corner and discussed our next move. About ten to fifteen minutes later, we heard another low rumble, louder than before. Within minutes, the FDNY radio confirmed what we already knew; there had been a partial collapse inside WTC 5.

John shook his head as if to say, *We dodged another bullet.*

"God, What Am I Going to Do with the Rest of My Life?"

I surveyed the intersection and watched as the professionals continued to bring order to the chaos. Then, I noticed something unusual: an actual functioning cell phone. I had not seen one all day. Prior to that moment, all communications around Ground Zero seemed to be destroyed, with the exception of handheld radios. I couldn't believe my eyes. Across the intersection was a firefighter talking into a cell phone. He was sweaty, beaten, and bloodied. Just like all of us.

As he spoke on the phone, I became a stalker. I walked toward the man, holding my distance at a respectful ten feet. I followed him as he walked and talked around the intersection. I was laser-locked on that phone. I needed that phone. My wife thought I was dead. I had to reach her. After several minutes, the firefighter said goodbye, and I was on top of him before he could even kill the connection.

"Hey, I need to use that phone" was my rude introduction. I realized my brutish ways and quickly pleaded my case. The guy didn't even let me finish as he handed me the phone.

I furiously dialed Heather's number and waited.

"Hi! You have reached Darin and Heather. We can't get to the phone right now." Are you kidding me? Voicemail! Correction: not voicemail but the answering machine. Remember those? Heather and I didn't own a cell phone at the time. I could only reach her by way of this mysterious relic from the past called a landline. Depending on your age, you may know this, but when no one was home to answer the landline, you left a voice message on a machine that literally included a micro audio cassette tape. Oh my, how technology has changed.

Anyway, I left a brief message on the machine. Honestly, I don't remember exactly what I said, but it was short and to the point. Most importantly, I wanted her to hear my voice and know I was still in the fight.

Now you may be thinking, *Where was his wife?* Thank you, so was I. Heather was a nurse at the time but Tuesday happened to be her day off. In a way, I wish she had been working because she wouldn't have been so isolated. But here's the deal. Heather was devastated. For Heather, my last known location was the lobby of the World Trade Center, and then thirteen minutes later, she watched it collapse. She cried, she prayed, and then she cried some more. She was engrossed in the media coverage, looking for a sign of hope. To make matters worse, she was receiving calls from well-meaning friends and family. Everyone wanted an update, but she had nothing to share. It was excruciating for her.

Finally, the four walls of our small apartment were closing in on her. She had to get out. Heather left and walked through town, traversing thirteen blocks until she found herself at the Hudson River waterfront. She walked out onto a grassy pier/park that lay almost exactly across the river from the smoldering ruins of the World Trade Center. Heather couldn't believe her eyes. It was gone. The entire complex was destroyed, shrouded in a murky haze of smoke and pulverized concrete.

That's when reality struck her in the face: "Darin is gone." She wept bitterly.

She prayed fervently. Heather sat for a few hours while staring across at the destruction. She prayed and lamented. At the young age of twenty-five, she already had her life "planned"—career, then children, then advanced degree, and so on. As she rose to her feet, Heather humbly asked God a simple question. "God, what am I going to do with the rest of my life?"

Thirteen blocks later, God allowed her at least a glimpse of the future. She entered the apartment to find the little red answering machine light blinking. *Great, more people with questions, and I have no answers*, she thought. She pressed the button, listened, and fell to her knees. I was alive.

"Thank you, Jesus!" she said out loud over and over. Heather knew hard times were coming, but she would not be asked to face them alone. We would press on together.

APPROXIMATELY 1500 HOURS, SEPTEMBER 11, 2001, CORNER OF CHURCH STREET AND VESEY STREET, NEW YORK CITY

After the phone call, I rejoined John and Rob on the block. We drank water while surveying the scene. In a sense, we were lost. We had fought the good fight and still had a lot of fight in us. But we couldn't seem to find a need we could address. The FDNY was swarming the area, and every time we tried to help, we kind of felt like we were in the way. The last thing we wanted to do was disrupt the rescue operations. I estimate we stood in the area for about twenty minutes before we began to get restless.

Then, suddenly, Frank appeared from nowhere. To this day, I'm still not sure where he had gone with the wounded couple or how he got back to our intersection. He just showed up and offered a solution to our dilemma. He had just found out, via his Secret Service handheld radio, the new location of the USSS emergency relocation area. Apparently, all USSS personnel were being asked to report to a location within the Chelsea Piers establishment along the Hudson River. This was about thirty blocks north of our intersection.

Then Frank called the three of us to huddle closer. "We heard back from Armas and Buckley [Tom and John]. They made it out OK. They're alive."

I pumped my fist and gritted out a "Yes!" while pushing back tears. I turned away from the group and silently wept. The emotions were overwhelming. I was convinced they were dead and overjoyed to be wrong. It was the first crack in the dam that was holding back my emotions. I quickly gathered myself and returned to the group. Then, we collectively decided to leave the area and report to the rendezvous spot.

Frank's car was on the street nearby. So, we limped our way a few blocks and folded our filthy bodies into his clean sedan. I collapsed in the back seat and closed my eyes. My fight for the day was done. Frank drove us out of the debris cloud and we collectively shielded our eyes from the oppressive sun. To my recollection, not a word was spoken as we sped north to reunite with our brothers and sisters.

CHAPTER 15

HOMECOMING

I believe everyone has a little hero in them. You gotta look in, and it's in there. It'll come out if it needs to.
—Robin Jones, engineer of the boat *Mary Gellatly*
(The Great Boat Lift of 9/11)

APPROXIMATELY 1530 HOURS, SEPTEMBER 11, 2001, CHELSEA PIERS, NEW YORK CITY

"Are you OK?" she asked.

I stared at her, unable to focus.

"Are you OK?" she repeated.

I snapped back into reality. "Yeah, good to go," I responded to the unknown medical personnel. And so, it began.

The four of us had walked from the car into a large commercial space in the Chelsea Piers complex. I can't speak for the others, but I guess I was in some state of shock. I surveyed the large bright room. It looked like the space was probably used for hosting private social events. There was a bar on the far end that looked oddly out of place, considering the circumstances. The room was quiet, with no words above a low murmur.

I glanced across the room and locked eyes with some good friends. I was happy to see them alive but also strangely numb to all emotions. The same unknown female quickly escorted us out a back door to an outside open area. Although we were walking and talking, we needed to be assessed medically. Other agents were already being tended to as I was guided to a seat.

To this day, this entire scene is a bit of a blur in my mind. An oxygen mask was attached to my face as an unknown medical team member began to assess me head to toe. I didn't have any significant injuries, just minor cuts and scrapes. Then, I was led to an irrigation station. I ripped off my tattered dress shirt and undershirt and held a water hose up to my eyes. I flushed them for several minutes and felt instant relief. I ran the hose over my head, scrubbing the soot and pulverized materials from my hair.

As I washed my face and arms, I began to feel human again. My clothes were trashed, so I carelessly doused my upper body with the hose in a desperate but futile attempt to wash away the stench of Ground Zero. Little did I know that stench would hover over lower Manhattan for weeks.

I figured I wasn't gonna look any better, so I dropped the hose and began to walk inside. Luckily, someone threw me a clean Chelsea Piers T-shirt as I entered the room. I glanced around the room and had only one thought: *I gotta get out of here*.

Suddenly, I didn't want to be around anyone. I was unreasonably irritable. In retrospect, I think I was simply finished. I was exhausted physically and emotionally. I had answered the bell, served with my brothers, and fought the good fight. Now, only one thing mattered. I needed to get home to Heather.

I looked across the Hudson River to Hoboken, New Jersey. From where I stood, I could almost see my apartment building. So close, yet so far. The island of Manhattan was shut down. The bridges and tunnels were closed. The subway and PATH trains were sealed off. There were only two ways off the island—walk or boat. Walking wasn't getting me to Jersey, but luckily a boat operation was already in the works. Another agent collected a list of colleagues who lived in New Jersey. Apparently, USSS agents from the Newark (NJ) Field Office were awaiting our arrival on the other side of the river. Once we crossed, they would transport us to our respective towns. All we needed was a boat.

I'm not sure who handled the logistics, but they deserve a ton of credit. Within half an hour, a Nassau County (Long Island) police boat moored itself to our dock. At least a dozen Secret Service agents wearily climbed aboard, and we pushed off: destination Weehawken, NJ.

The Great Boat Lift of 9/11

The crew and passengers of our tiny vessel were part of history in the making. They, like me, just didn't know it at the time. The pilot and crew of our police boat were members of a herculean effort never seen before in modern history. I'm a former history teacher. Therefore, I can't resist. In 1940, the invading German blitzkrieg was ripping through Western Europe like a buzz saw. By May, the remaining French, Belgian, and English forces were in danger of being trapped as they were cut off by the German armored divisions. At the Battle of Dunkirk, the Allies pulled off the unthinkable. In just nine days, 339,000 Allied troops were successfully evacuated from northern France to the safe shores of the United Kingdom. While under constant barrage, eight hundred vessels, small and large, completed the largest amphibious evacuation in military history. While it was a devastating defeat, the Allied armies lived to fight another day.

It's difficult to comprehend, but the historic success at Dunkirk was eclipsed on September 11, 2001. During and after the initial attack, civilians began fleeing toward the waterways for escape. Shortly after the second tower collapsed, an emergency distress call was issued by the United States Coast Guard. The USCG commander on the scene grabbed his radio and said the following: "All available boats, this is the United States Coast Guard aboard the pilot boat *New York*. Any boat willing to help with the evacuation of lower Manhattan, report to Governor's Island."

The response was overwhelming. Within minutes, all sorts of vessels descended on the rally point. Ferry boats, military boats, tug boats, and recreational vessels of all sorts converged in the waters of lower Manhattan. The call went out, and *citizens* answered the bell! Over 150 vessels took part in the operation. The Great Boat Lift of 9/11 became the largest sea evacuation in history.

In nine hours, approximately half a million civilians were evacuated via boat from lower Manhattan. Read that sentence again. And now, review the stats from Dunkirk. How is this possible? Because over six hundred pilots and sailors, citizens of a republic, did their duty and answered the call for their countrymen. You want 9/11 heroes? Here's six hundred more. Such selfless service in the face of danger is the embodiment of the American spirit, which makes our nation exceptional.

Our boat pulled alongside a nondescript dock in Wee-hawken, New Jersey. Waiting to receive us were several stunned Special Agents from our Newark Field Office. I guess we looked like zombies because the Newark agents didn't say much, and we were in no mood for chit chat. But they were a huge blessing. They called out their assigned destinations in Jersey, and the New York agents began shuffling to their respective cars.

Fortunately for me, Hoboken was only about five minutes south. Again, the car ride was eerily quiet. I lived in the north end of town, so I think my apartment was the first stop. I thanked the driver and locked eyes with my New York broth-ers: "See y'all tomorrow." Maybe a funny thing to say? We didn't know what "tomorrow" would bring. But my brothers and I knew "tomorrow" would bring a new mission and a new opportunity to contribute to America's new war.

APPROXIMATELY 1635 HOURS, SEPTEMBER 11, 2001, WASHINGTON STREET, HOBOKEN, NEW JERSEY

I had gone to work that morning in a crisp suit, carrying a gym bag and my everyday gear backpack. I walked across the sidewalk that afternoon carrying nothing, wearing a new T-shirt, tattered suit pants with holes, and destroyed dress shoes with melted soles.

A young mother pushing a baby stroller passed in front of me. A look of disbelief covered her face. "God bless you" was all she could kindly offer.

I walked up two steps, braced my hands against the glass door, and took in a deep breath. I had lost my keys at some point, so I pushed the call button for apartment 3.

"Darin?" Heather's voice crackled from the speaker.

"It's me, honey." The door unlocked, and I quickly ascended two flights of stairs, the last stairs of my day.

As I reached for the knob, the door opened.

"I'm OK" was all I could utter before the tidal wave of emotions sent me into Heather's arms. I had fought, bled, and nearly died twice. I had given my very substance to my fellow Service brothers and the citizens of New York. In the aftermath, I had lived in the foggy haze of adrenaline crash and shock. Once the "mission" was complete, I had turned my attention to the next objective. Just get home. Throughout it all, I had kept my emotions in check. In Heather's arms, the dam broke.

She spoke in my ear. "I love you. I love you. I love you." We both wept uncontrollably. We literally fell to the floor and held each other as we sobbed. Was it pain, joy, or both? This was no Hollywood scene. We didn't passionately kiss and promise to never be apart again. No, this was a vortex of primal agony and joy cascading through tears, snot, and weeping drool. Gross but beautiful.

I needed a shower. Heather handed me a kitchen trash bag as I entered the bathroom. I peeled off my melted shoes and tattered clothes, placing them in the trash bag. I tied a knot around the bag and just stared at it. Later, I placed the bag in the back corner of our large walk-in closet.

There it would sit, for years. I just couldn't throw it away.

I climbed in the shower and began the longest, best shower of my life. I felt like I showered for an hour. I cried, I prayed, and I asked God, "Why?" The hot water washed away the grime, but it could not wash me clean of the memories.

It could not wash away the pain. It could not answer my questions. But Jesus could do all that—in time.

Embrace of Grace

I made this point earlier in chapter 6, but it's one we cannot hear enough. I believe the scene of Heather and me reuniting serves as a beautiful illustration of a foundational biblical truth. When Heather opened the door and laid her eyes on me, what did she see? A broken man. I looked disgusting. Despite my attempts at washing, I was still bruised, bloodied, and covered head to toe in filth. My pants were shredded, each leg about three inches shorter than before. My shoes were destroyed, barely staying on my feet. But probably most notably, my face revealed my pain and anguish. In short, I was a complete mess.

What did Heather do? She embraced me. Now, if I had walked in the door covered head to toe in mud from a rough tackle football game, she would have backed away and pointed to the shower.

"Don't touch me," she would declare as she gave me "the Heisman" to my chest. But that wasn't the case.

Here's the facts: I was filthy. I was broken. And she loved me anyway. Therefore, she hugged me, brought me close, joined in my pain, and wept with me. At that moment, I began to heal. Now, multiply that experience by a billion. My friends, this scene beautifully captures our condition as we all approach Jesus for the first time. In the biblical scenario, we are broken and filthy in our own sin. Heck, the Bible says, in that condition separated from God, even our good deeds are like filthy rags (Isaiah 64:6). Yet, when we turn to Jesus, everything changes.

"Turning to Jesus" simply means this: confessing with your mouth that Jesus is Lord and actually believing it in your heart. Bam! What follows is a confession of sin and turning away from it. Your heart of stone becomes a heart of flesh as you become a new creation. But please do not miss my point. Jesus does not require us to fix ourselves and clean ourselves up before we come to him. It's the exact opposite; He takes us as we are. I call it the "Embrace of Grace."

The tear-filled embrace between Heather and me was powerful. But it's not even a shadow of the embrace Jesus offers us all.

1730 HOURS, SEPTEMBER 11, 2001, WASHINGTON STREET, HOBOKEN, NEW JERSEY

Clean from my shower, I stood in the living room and couldn't believe my eyes. I stared at the TV as I watched WTC 7, my office building, collapse. In a weird way, I was almost emotionless. I had nothing left.

Heather and I held hands as I asked aloud, "What will I do tomorrow?"

CHAPTER 16

NEW DAY, NEW MISSION

No battle plan survives contact with the enemy.
—Field Marshal Helmuth von Moltke

WEDNESDAY, SEPTEMBER 12, 2001, WASHINGTON STREET, HOBOKEN, NEW JERSEY

To this day, my mind is blank. It's as if the long hot shower on the evening of 9/11 served as a mind eraser. I'm sure an expert could provide an explanation, but I am at a loss. I have almost zero memory from the evening of 9/11 to the early afternoon of 9/12. Within that time gap, I have one simple recollection. Heather asked what my plan was for the day.

"I have no idea" was my flat response. Then she gave me some very sound advice.

Heather said, "You need to write your experience down, all of it, now." So, I did. I fired up the computer on our desk and began to type. The result was a detailed account of my 9/11 experience, totaling five pages, single-spaced. Today, I have two paper copies. In a way, that document serves as the foundation of this book, just the facts. I am grateful to have it and I will be sure to pass it on to my sons in due time. I guess I need to make two more copies.

Other than my wife's writing assignment, I have no other memories of the morning and early afternoon. I simply couldn't watch the news coverage, so the apartment was quiet. Later in the afternoon, an informal gathering was arranged. At least a dozen Secret Service agents lived in Hoboken at the time. We all agreed to get together at the apartment owned by my colleague, Tim.

I walked a few blocks south to Tim's apartment, not knowing what to expect. I opened the door and was immediately disappointed to see the news playing on the TV. I wanted to escape from the news coverage. The room was crowded but eerily quiet, which was great because I didn't feel like talking. The mood was solemn, yet I felt a sense of comfort being with my guys.

I distanced myself from the TV and began small talk with other colleagues as beers started to be passed around. The scene became extremely awkward. None of us knew what to do. The United States had just been sucker punched in the face, and we felt helpless. A dozen alpha males sat in the living room, stewing in our emotions. As the afternoon continued, we stared at the TV in near silence. We were hurt. We were pissed. We were motivated. But we were without a mission.

Then everything changed. Breaking news.

The news anchor began their new lead story. Someone grabbed the remote and turned up the volume. It sounded something like this: "The White House has just confirmed President Bush will visit the World Trade Center site in New York City this Friday." We watched the report with intense focus. As the news anchor transitioned to the next story, Tim immediately killed the TV feed with the remote. I vividly remember what happened next.

"That's it, boys," Tim said. "We gotta job to do." To a man, beers were dumped in the trash, hugs exchanged, and everyone departed to get some sleep. I walked home with a refound purpose in my step. "My guys" and I had a new mission. The President of the United States (POTUS) was visiting our city, and it was literally a war zone. My body was beaten and bruised, but my mind was clear.

Tomorrow, we prepare. Friday, we execute.

THURSDAY, SEPTEMBER 13, 2001, AN UNDISCLOSED BUILDING AT JFK INTERNATIONAL AIRPORT, JAMAICA, NEW YORK

One by one, vehicles of all sorts filtered into a nondescript parking lot at JFK International Airport. New York Field Office (NYFO) agents arrived mostly via their personally owned vehicles because a majority of our government vehicles (mine included) were buried in the rubble beneath the World Trade Center.

Every agent in the New York district had been notified to rally at an empty warehouse on the edge of the airport. POTUS was due to arrive in less than twenty-four hours, and we were not prepared. The day turned out to be a "family reunion" blended with a high-stakes business meeting and a little operational briefing sprinkled on top. We even threw in a quick therapy session too. Just another day at the office.

Oh yeah, we also almost had a rebellion.

All the USSS personnel gathered inside, with some standing and some sitting on folding chairs. The warehouse was poorly lit, dusty, and had a musky smell. It definitely had not been used in years. There was a buzz of excitement in the air. Collectively, we were pumped to be gearing up for a mission. Everyone was eager to learn the operational plans. Personally, I was thankful to have a distraction from the madness and ready to get on with the mission.

The room suddenly grew quiet as the Special Agent in Charge (SAIC) of the New York Field Office began to address the agents. No one remembers what he said to begin, but everyone remembers his closing remarks. He informed us that "headquarters" had decided the POTUS visit would be handled by agents from nearby Newark, New Jersey, and Boston, Massachusetts. The New York agents were to stand down because we had "suffered enough stress already."

The reaction was instant and brutal.

Screams of "This is bulls——t!" and "Hell, no!" were launched in the first salvo. Everyone began to shout down the SAIC. He probably felt like a Red Sox fan in the bleacher seats at Yankee Stadium. But our message was clear to the leadership: there was no way we were going to let "outside" agents handle our mission. It was a principle worth fighting over, and we were all looking to scrap.

At the time, we were the largest field office in the country. We always took tremendous pride in that we could handle a POTUS and VPOTUS visit in the same week with zero assistance from other offices. We referred to ourselves as "the Flagship." Does that sound arrogant? Yes. But we were good, and we knew it. It was time to rise to the challenge, not shrink into self-pity. Eventually, the SAIC wisely retreated from his position and said he would state our case to HQ. We took that as a win.

The room began to settle down as we expected to receive the operational briefing. Sadly, that was not next on the agenda. The Secret Service had dutifully brought in grief/trauma counselors to meet with the agents. Most of us just wanted to prepare for the next day's mission, but it was made clear that group counseling was not voluntary. Bring on the awkwardness! We broke into groups according to our investigative squads.

At the counselor's direction, we formed a large circle of about twenty chairs, and she sat in the middle. Each agent sat quietly in their seats, awkwardly staring at the tops of their shoes. The counselor began to facilitate the "conversation." Don't get me wrong. I believe professional counseling and group therapy can help make monumental progress for one's mental health. But there is a time and a place, and this was neither. We just wanted to get back in the fight, do the next thing, and attack the next mission as a team. But first, we had to do the "struggle session."

The session began, and unfortunately, I was one of the first to speak. Allow myself to make fun of . . . myself, again. The prompt was simple: "Share your experience from Tuesday." Well, I like to talk. Shocking, I know. So, I jumped right in, telling my story from the beginning. According to witnesses, I talked for a while. Those same witnesses would proceed to make fun of me for years. I now recall Will Ferrell's character in *Old School* during his counseling session: "What? I thought we were in the trust tree?"

Anyway, I finally wrapped it up, and other agents shared their experiences. I was embarrassed when each agent took only about a minute. At least, they were smart enough to be short and to the point. We wrapped up the session, and honestly, I thought it was helpful. But we still wanted to get on with business.

The frustration and nervous energy in the building was about to boil over. Everyone was thinking the same thing: *Let us do our job!* Finally, the SAIC regained the attention of the entire forum. The room went quiet. To our delight, he informed us that upon further consideration, the New York Field Office was back in business. We would handle all aspects of the POTUS visit the following day. With our final hurdle cleared, we all moved forward with our objectives. There was no time to waste.

Immediately, the wheels of the protective advance began to turn. Someone unknown to me managed to pull off a logistic miracle. In less than forty-eight hours, US military assets had airlifted tons of spare USSS protective equipment to New York. American exceptionalism at its finest. I received a new handgun, radio, handcuffs, and other protective gear. Other long weapons were distributed, and new cars were rolled into the lot.

My friend Brian and I were assigned a car to share since we lived a block from each other in Hoboken. The cars were less than ideal. Although they were new, most were cheap, boxy sedans from the federal General Services Administration (GSA). Not exactly the same as our cool "undercover" cars or muscular police-style interceptors. And then there was the cherry on top. Each GSA car had government GSA license plates. The plates literally read "US Government." I guess we weren't going to use those in a surveillance operation. That being said, the cars were a little embarrassing but understandable, considering the circumstances. We were very grateful just to have four wheels.

The logistics train kept running as everyone continued to retool and refit. By the time it was complete, we rallied together again to receive our assignment for the following day. Our leaders called out names, and we began to form up in groups. As our leader briefed us on our assignment, I couldn't believe what was happening. I was stunned, scared, and pumped up beyond belief, all at the same time. I was assigned to work the arrival of POTUS at the Ground Zero site. Specifically, the president was set to arrive at the site near the intersection of Church Street and Vesey Street. I was returning to my battlefield. I couldn't think of a better place to get back in the fight.

But my supervisor had other ideas. Apparently, I had shared too much in our group counseling session. In his mind, I had experienced too much trauma just two days prior, especially at Church and Vesey. Once he heard of my assignment, he made his decision.

"Kinder, I'm pulling you off that site. I'll find another job for you to do." Keep in mind, at the time, I was a punk twenty-seven-year-old, very junior "Not-So-Special Agent." This guy was a no-nonsense older veteran. As he turned to leave, I touched him on the arm and spoke with an authority I did not rightfully possess.

"Absolutely not, sir," I said. "That's exactly where I need to be. Come on, boss."

I guess I was convincing, or perhaps he had bigger issues to deal with. He relented with a grunt and wave of the hand. Friday was gonna be one heck of an experience.

FRIDAY, SEPTEMBER 14, 2001, GROUND ZERO, NEW YORK CITY

Here we go again. I surveyed the scene, taking in the visual destruction and smell of carnage. The smell was sharp, pungent, and impossible to escape. To this day, I refer to it as the smell of death. The overcast skies matched the mood on the ground. Even three days later, the heaping rubble smoldered with smoke and gas. Burned-out empty hulks of vehicles littered the street. The thick air and cluttered ground were both damp. The overcast skies matched the mood on the ground. The intersection was a beehive of activity. Construction workers and rescue personnel crawled all over the scene. I was standing in the same area I had served in all day on 9/11.

But now, I felt oddly out of place. A tear formed in my eye. Wiping it away, I took a deep breath and stuffed the emotions deep down. There was a time to deal with issues of pain and loss. This moment was not the time. That was it. The rest of my experience on September 14, 2001, was all business.

Let me put all the cards on the table. I will approach this section of my story with great care. I'll be very careful about what I share. I will not be discussing any of the USSS's protective methodologies employed that day. I will not divulge plans, methods, and tactics. I will not discuss logistics, intelligence assets, and contingency plans. I will only provide you a firsthand account of my experience, from only my perspective. If you want a comprehensive look into the Secret Service's actions on September 14, 2001, I suggest you Google it.

I also don't want to exaggerate my role in the mission of September 14. Keep in mind: I was a very junior agent at the time. The protective advance and other heavy lifting were conducted by more senior agents. I was simply told to be at the corner of the West Side Highway and Vesey Street in the predawn hours of September 14.

That being said, the day was unforgettable for many reasons, which I'll discuss. September 11, 2001, was the worst day of my life. However, September 14, 2001, may be the most impactful day of my professional career.

The entire area was crawling with rescue workers, including firefighters, cops, steel cutters, construction workers, and EMS personnel. The scene resembled a loose pattern of organized chaos. What struck me the most was everyone was working with a unified purpose toward one objective: free survivors from the rubble. These men and women were answering the bell every day in the slim hope that others might live. Hope was in the air, but so was righteous anger.

I could smell it. I could feel it.

We met early in a large group along the West Side Highway. The group consisted of USSS agents, NYPD officers, and even a few state troopers. It was unlike any protective briefing I have ever received because we were on the edge of a very active rescue and recovery operation. Therein lies the challenge of the day. How do we secure this entire area for POTUS while not hindering rescue operations? If that sounds impossible to you, then you would be correct. Regardless, we received our briefing, and we each walked around to our respective posts of duty. After all the agents and officers were posted up, we were ready for the arrival of POTUS. Or so we thought.

I opened this chapter with a well-known quote from one of the great military minds of the nineteenth century, Prussian

Field Marshal Helmuth von Moltke. It's a condensed quotation from some of his more extensive writings on military tactics and strategy. The basic idea was that an army should plan for a battle, but it also must have layers of flexibility built into its system because the enemy rarely reacts as anticipated.

Although I respect von Moltke, I prefer the even more succinct take on this concept from one of boxing's all-time greats. According to Iron Mike Tyson, "Everyone has a plan until they get punched in the face."

We had a plan to secure the Ground Zero site. Then we got punched in the face.

The "enemy," in this case, was reality. There had been no time for a proper protective advance, and the site was an active search-and-rescue operation crowded with men and women trying to do their jobs. By the time POTUS arrived, our outer and middle perimeters were shrinking back. To make matters more challenging, POTUS arrived with New York Governor George Pataki and New York City Mayor Rudy Giuliani. Everyone who was anyone was there, and they were all jockeying for position next to the president. It was nearly impossible to maintain a secure perimeter.

It wasn't long before the agents formed a tight perimeter around the entire party, not just POTUS. We were pushing and shoving "important" people out of the way as we struggled to hold our ground. That's when I glanced over my shoulder to see the president a mere ten feet away. This was not supposed to be my position. It is 100 percent not normal for such a junior agent to be that close to the president. But this was no ordinary day.

Bloodlust in the Air

The entourage slowly made its way beyond the outer edges of the site when a peculiar phenomenon happened. President Bush began to interact with the rescue workers face to face. This was not the plan as I remember it.

Immediately, the chaotic scene became eerily quiet. It was as if everyone was following a prearranged agreement. This was hallowed ground. Show your respect with quiet reverence. Now, the agents found themselves working an impromptu "rope line" with the rescue workers. I've worked on countless rope lines in my career. You have all seen them on TV, even the movies. The president concludes remarks at a political rally and then descends from the stage to methodically shake hands with attendees in the first couple of rows. The attendees are often VIPs with exclusive access to the front row, or they are super committed devotees who got in line hours before anyone else. These people often gush over the president, gratuitously heaping praise on their political "savior." That's a normal rope line. But this was different.

This makeshift rope line was not made of wealthy political donors. It was "Tony," the firefighter from Brooklyn; "Sal," the steamfitter hailing from Queens; "Frank," the construction worker from Jersey. These were hard men doing hard work. And they were angry, not at the president but rather at the terrorists and those who supported them. They wanted revenge, and they made it very clear to their president. I can't repeat most of what they said because it was pretty vulgar. But it was also genuine, visceral, and personal.

Many of the roughnecks addressed the president by his first name. Imagine a firefighter from Brooklyn telling the president of the United States, "George, you make those mother——s pay for this!" I was within earshot, so I can tell you this happened repeatedly as he walked down the line. Later in my career, I heard President Bush himself describe this situation, and he referred to the "bloodlust" in the air. Bloodlust perfectly describes the tone and attitude I witnessed on September 14.

One by one, the exhausted rescue workers charged their president to seek justice or revenge, whichever came first. I rarely publicly voice my opinion on politics, but I'll dip my toe into political waters for just a moment. I witnessed greatness on September 14. I watched the common man come face to face with their elected leader. I witnessed many "average Joe" Americans demand action from their president. And I had a front-row seat as the leader of the free world entered into the pain of his people. He listened; he received. And he made a promise. That promise was two-fold: Justice will be served, and I will never let this happen again. I have no way of knowing for sure, but I believe President Bush's personal interactions that day served as the driving force of his commitment to victory in the war on terror.

I scanned the crowd as we progressed down the line. The crowd began to chant, "USA! USA! USA!" The hair on the back of my neck stood up. What followed was something from a Hollywood script. We formed a makeshift perimeter around an elevated pile of debris as President Bush climbed on top. I was mere feet from the president as he was joined by FDNY firefighter Bob Beckwith. In an impromptu moment of compassion and true grit, President Bush grabbed a bullhorn to address the raucous crowd before him.

As the president began to speak, multiple rescue workers cried out, "We can't hear you!"

President Bush responded with these iconic words: "I can hear you. The rest of the world hears you. And the people who knocked these buildings down will hear all of us soon!"

The rescue workers went nuts. "USA! USA! USA!" On September 14, 2001, America's leader modeled justice and compassion with fierce intensity. I was honored to witness history, and deep down, I committed myself to the same fight. I realized at that moment that justice and compassion were not mutually exclusive. I decided the rest of my days on this earth would be defined by the same virtues.

CHAPTER 17

TIME TO GET DIRTY

*Besides this you know the time, that the hour has come
for you to wake up from sleep. For salvation is nearer
to us now than when we first believed. The night is
far gone; the day is at hand. So then let us cast off the
works of darkness and put on the armor of light.*
—Romans 13:11–12

Are you ready to get dirty? I have a confession to make. Earlier, I purposefully skipped part of my story. It appeared I walked you through the entirety of my personal experience of September 11, 2001. But that's not exactly the case. I intentionally hit the fast-forward button on the scene at Chelsea Piers because my desire is for this point to stand alone. I want it to hit you square in the face like a clean left hook.

To review, I, along with my three brothers-in-arms, traveled via car to the final Secret Service rendezvous point of the day. We arrived at Chelsea Piers on the West Side Highway as a ragtag group. We were beaten, bloodied, and marred by the fight. We entered a large commercial space to rally up with our colleagues.

As I entered the room, I quickly surveyed the scene. An unknown female was trying to push us quickly out the back to receive a medical evaluation and a change of clothes. But I stopped and locked eyes with several "brothers" in the room. On the right side of the room was a large group of agents, and they looked very similar to me, John, Rob, and Frank. To put it mildly, they were in rough shape. Clothes were in tatters, and their faces were covered in soot and ash.

We gave each other subtle nods and a slight wink, conveying an unspoken message: *Well done, you fought the good fight.*

Then, my eyes drifted left to the far side of the space. I gazed upon another group of agents. I was confused, maybe a little stunned.

My shell-shocked mind was slow to compute. They appeared different. Because they were. They were clean. Their suits were spotless, shoes were shiny, and their faces and hair were perfect.

Our newly arrived ragtag group of four was receiving the same shocked and confused looks in return from the far side of the room. I could see it on their faces. It was as if an animated quotation bubble were visible over their heads. It read "Where have you been?"

It's funny because the exact same question was forming in my mind. *No, where have you been!*

Both groups stared at each other in disbelief. I slightly shook my head and made my way to the back door. *Where the hell have they been?* I asked myself again as I left the space.

Earlier, in chapter 12, we dissected a simple truth. Courage is a choice. The actions of many on September 11, 2001, proved no different. We have already honored the firefighters and first responders who answered the bell despite their awareness of the dire facts on the ground. They made a choice. We also parsed the difference between a civilian and a citizen. The citizens of September 11, 2001, entered into the fray to help their fellow man. They made a choice.

The "clean suits" at Chelsea Piers also made a choice. They chose self-preservation, comfort, and safety. I do not know the circumstances of each individual in that room. I do not know the options from which they had to choose. But I do know one thing.

They were clean. They were unmarked.

The question is why. Or, you may be asking, *Why not?* Let me be very clear. I do not mention this group of colleagues to disparage anyone's character. I have zero malice in my heart toward them. My desire is not to add shame or embarrassment to anyone's conscience. And I certainly will not belittle a group of people who went on to bravely serve their nation for decades in a dangerous capacity. Their service deserves our respect. I bring up the "clean suits" only to make a much larger point. I want to use the image of the "clean suits" as an illustration to challenge and encourage men to answer the bell.

Get Your Suit Dirty

In the months and years following September 11, 2001, I struggled mightily with a sense of lost purpose. The Lord led me out of that darkness by placing His will for my life and giving me clarity in my heart. But it didn't take me years to see the dichotomy between the "clean suits" and the "dirty suits." In fact, it took less than a day. On the afternoon of September 12, 2001, I sat silently in my living room sipping coffee. I couldn't get the image of the agents in clean suits out of my mind. It baffled me. I kept asking myself, *Where the hell were they?*

But then, in that moment, God released me from the question. It's as if he smacked me on the back of the head and said, "You're missing the point, you dolt!" The image carries weight and meaning: "Don't be a clean suit!"

That's it. You know, by now, I like to keep it simple. Men, here is my challenge to you. Spend the rest of your days getting your "suit" dirty for the glory of God. Don't be a "clean suit." Each day, we make a choice. Just like courage is a choice, getting "dirty" is a choice.

It means intentionally entering into the pain and suffering of others. It means choosing to confront the problems of this world. It means choosing to be an agent of light in this present darkness. It means speaking and living with the authority of your Creator as an ambassador for Christ. It means service over self.

It means exposing ourselves to the hard things of life and gritting our teeth as we lift up our fellow brothers and sisters. It means being the man who valiantly "quells the storm and rides the thunder." It means moving forward with a full heart of courage as you embrace the promises and command of John 16:33: "In the world you will have tribulation. But take heart; I have overcome the world."

A life of "getting dirty" for Jesus will be hard. It will have challenges. And it can only be powered by love, God's love for you, which is reflected back out to others in your sphere of influence. It will be scary, and you will want to run. But the opposite of fear is love, God's love. It's perfect, it's powerful, and it casts out all fear.

This may sound great to you. You're thinking; *I'm fired up by this. I want to get my suit dirty.* The question I have for you is "When?" Men, the answer is "Now."

"You do not know what tomorrow will bring. What is your life? For you are a mist that appears for a little time and then vanishes" (James 4:14). Our days are numbered. This entire 9/11 story makes that point very clear. We can go at any time. When I receive the "upward call," when I punch out of this world, bury me in a dirty suit. I want the same for you. Your wife, children, and friends want the same for you. The night has gone. The day has come. Now arm up for the fight of the day. The time is now. Do not be afraid. God and the love of Jesus will be your strength.

"Fear not, O Zion; let not your hands grow weak. The Lord your God is in your midst, a mighty one who will save; he will rejoice over you with gladness; he will quiet you by his love; he will exult over you with loud singing" (Zephaniah 3:16–17). I'll share one of my key objectives for this life. When I die, I want my loved ones to gather and share stories about my selfless service. I'm not perfect, nor ever will be. But my desire is to make a mark on the people I encounter. I want them to see and feel the love of Jesus through me.

Bury Me in a Dirty Suit

It would be a shame if you left this world in a clean suit. Maybe you once fought but at some point thought, *No más.* Or maybe you never entered the ring at all. Only a fighter knows the agony of receiving a punch to the ribs but also the joy of landing a clean right hook. The Enemy, through the power of sin, wreaks havoc in this domain. What if you woke up every morning with the mindset of creating trouble, good trouble, for the Enemy?

This world is full of problems. You were created to be a solution for at least one. Answer the bell. Get back in the fight. Get your suit dirty. Then you can look the Enemy in the eye, give him a grin, and boldly declare, "Everyone has a plan until they get punched in the face."

PART IV

THE (UN)SAFE LIFE

CHAPTER 18

NO SAFE SPACES

"Aslan is a lion—the Lion, the great Lion."
*"Ooh!" said Susan. "I'd thought he was a man. Is he—quite
safe? I shall feel rather nervous about meeting a lion."*
. . .
*"Safe?" said Mr. Beaver . . . "Who said anything about safe?
'Course he isn't safe. But he's good. He's the King, I tell you."*
— C. S. Lewis, *The Lion, the Witch, and the Wardrobe*

We live in troubled times. Violence, economic uncertainty, racial strife, zero-sum politics, and past global pandemics are just a few of the problems polluting the air we breathe. Because of this, our society has become obsessed with "being safe."

"Be safe" and "Stay safe" are mantras stuck on repeat in our minds, rolling off our tongues with ease. Do me a favor. Start paying attention to how many times you hear some iteration of "Be safe" and "Stay safe" in your day-to-day living. It is staggering. It makes me cringe when someone cheerfully says, "Safety first." I just want to punch them. Not really. Well, maybe.

I push back against that mindset at every opportunity, sometimes sarcastically. When my teenage sons leave the house, my wife almost often tells them to "drive safe," which is reasonable. But before the front door closes, I'll yell, "Drive fast and take chances, son." Oddly, she's never found it funny.

Modernity has deemed all kinds of things "unsafe": words, opposing ideas, silent prayers. In fact, words are actually violence. I could go on, but I'll spare us all. Therefore, some demand "safe spaces" to protect themselves from opposing ideas. But let's say goodbye to the coloring books and stuffed animals as we leave the safe spaces behind and enter into the "real world." Let us boldly run headlong into the (un)safe life!

At its fundamental core, we live in a culture feeding on fear. The foundation of the fear is conflict. The subterranean bedrock of that conflict is sin. The bottom line is we are a rebellious race (humanity) who turned its back on God's perfect created order. Christians, this is where we live. But there is hope. "In the world you will have tribulation. But take heart; I have overcome the world." (John 16:33).

I've quoted this verse twice now because it's simple and so true. It contains one command sandwiched by two promises. The first promise is life will be hard; that's a fact. Then comes the command: have courage. Why? Because "I have overcome the world" is the second promise. This refers to the smashing victory in Christ we all possess as believers in Him. Sometimes, life is just plain hard. And that will be the case until Christ's return. In the space between, we are called to advance in life toward our God-given purpose, a life driven by love, not fear. That's the (un)safe life.

Why call it the (un)safe life? Allow me to explain. What seems "unsafe" to the secular culture is actually the safest place to be. How is that possible? Because we have allowed the culture to redefine *safe*. Dictionary.com defines *safe* as "secure from liability to harm, injury, danger, or risk." Our modern culture has changed *safe* to be synonymous with "comfortable." Let's tease this out even further. In modern times, *safe* means comfort, the absence of opposition, compliance with the majority, affirmation of all ideas. And furthermore, our feelings are "our truth." Therefore, if I *feel* unsafe, then I am in danger.

The Coddling of the American Mind is a brilliant book written by Greg Lukiannoff and Jonathan Haidt. The book dissects how some good-intentioned policies on college campuses are making young Americans incredibly fragile. It opens with a fictitious story about the authors traveling to Greece to mine the wisdom of a reclusive oracle. The oracle, hilariously named Misoponos (meaning "a hater of painful toil and hardship"), enlightens them with a couple of wisdom bombs. One is "What doesn't kill you makes you weaker," and the other is "Always trust your feelings. Never question them." The rest of the book is dedicated to debunking those two incredible lies, as well as others. I highly recommend the read, even if it's a sad fact the book actually needed to be written.

We may snicker at the silliness of what our culture defines as safe, but the American Christian church is following the culture's lead, not vice versa. Comfort is king, Walk into most American churches and you'll find the perfect coffee, donuts, light and smoke shows, most times paired with a soft positive message from the pulpit: be nice, be loving, be liked, avoid conflict, never cause trouble. Keep everyone comfortable. All the while, the church has to beg its members, especially the men, to serve in some capacity. Afterward, we shake hands, leave the building, and walk defenseless into a busted and broken world that's looking for someone to devour. My friend Andy often laments that each church should be its own little battleship, but most of them are just cruise ships. Everyone wants to be comfortable.

The results are catastrophic. Instead of being the light, pointing people to the light, or being ambassadors for Christ, we become just like the culture. Therefore, we hesitate to speak boldly about our faith because it may cost us friends, degrade our social status, or get us "in trouble" in the workplace. We are timid to stand firm on the Scriptures because it may make us look weird or sound unloving. We choose to avoid engaging with evil because it will make us uncomfortable.

So, I offer this rebuttal: What if Jesus were only nice? Imagine if Jesus was obsessed with being liked. What if Jesus was never in conflict and never caused trouble? What if Jesus never attacked evil? Then, he would not be worthy of our worship because he would have never gone to the cross. He would have lived a safe life as a "nice guy," a successful carpenter, with many casual friends, while dying quietly and being buried in a clean suit.

But he didn't. Because that was not the will of His Father. Jesus lived a hard life, oftentimes without a place to lay his head (Matthew 8:20). Jesus spoke truth to power, usually creating trouble for him and his followers (Matthew 23:23–28). Jesus chose to cast out demons, heal the sick, and even raise the dead. He chose to enter the fray. All of which made him a threat in the eyes of the religious leaders of the day (John 11:45–57). Ultimately, he willingly drove a dagger through the heart of evil as he conquered death by way of his death and resurrection.

Safe to say, Jesus was never comfortable. But he was always safe because there is no safer place to be than the center of God's will.

Safety Is Not a Calling

So, here's the problem I want to address. Most Christians, especially the men, spend their lives seeking safety and comfort instead of seeking the will of God. Pursuing and actively living out the will of God leads to a life of joy, contentment, and fulfillment while bringing glory and honor to God. As I mentioned in chapter 3, safety and comfort are often not part of His plan. Men, hear me clearly. Safe is boring. Safe is comfortable. Safe is lazy. Safe doesn't strike fear in the heart of the Enemy. God does not call us to play it safe. I want to call you up to a life in which you valiantly execute God's perfect purpose for your life. But before we get there, we need to become "comfortable" with, not fearful of, the fact that we live in a fallen world of conflict and we have a righteous warrior God Who hates sin and evil.

God is love. God is fierce. God is perfect righteousness. God is justice. Therefore, it's important to examine and worship all aspects of God the Father. In the modern evangelical church, we often focus exclusively on God's attributes of love and compassion, and rightfully so. However, when we do this, we miss out on the balanced totality of the Lord Almighty. I highlight the warrior aspects of God, not to elevate it above others, but to draw attention to this often-neglected aspect of Him.

The Scriptures are clear that God is also a fierce warrior who battles on behalf of his people. In the book of Exodus, the Israelites were fleeing from Pharaoh's army as they closed the distance to their camp with their backs to the Red Sea. Then Moses reminded his people they were not called to "safe" themselves:

> And Moses said to the people, "Fear not, stand firm, and see the salvation of the Lord, which he will work for you today. For the Egyptians whom you see today, you shall never see again. *The Lord will fight for you* [my emphasis], and you have only to be silent." (Exodus 14:13–14)

The Lord brought destruction on Pharaoh's army as they were swallowed by the Red Sea. Therefore, Moses and the people of Israel sang the following:

> The Lord is my strength and my song, and He has become my salvation;
> this is my God, and I will praise Him, my father's God, and I will exalt Him.
> *The Lord is a man of war* [my emphasis]; the Lord is His name. (Exodus 15:2–3)

This is the kind of God we worship:

> The Lord goes out like a mighty man, like a man of war. He stirs up his zeal;
> He cries out, He shouts aloud, He shows himself mighty against His foes. (Isaiah 43:13)

The New Testament also echoes the warrior ethos that makes up part of God the Father. And it calls out the followers of Christ to engage evil in our world:

> For we do not wrestle against flesh and blood, but against the rulers, against the authorities, against the cosmic powers over this present darkness, against the spiritual forces of evil in the heavenly places. Therefore take up the whole armor of God, that you may be able to withstand in the evil day, and having done all, to stand firm. (Ephesians 6:12–13)

Last, in the final days, the Bible paints an epic picture of Jesus's return. This is not the pale-skinned, soft, shampoo-model Jesus that many people have painted over the years. This is Jesus as a warrior, leading an army, armed with a sword, and entering battle wearing a bloody robe:

> Then I saw heaven opened, and behold, a white horse! The one sitting on it is called Faithful and True, and in righteousness he judges and makes war. His eyes are like a flame of fire, and on his head are many diadems, and he has a name written that no one knows but himself. He is clothed in a robe dipped in blood, and the name by which he is called is The Word of God. And the armies of heaven, arrayed in fine linen, white and pure, were following him on white horses. From his mouth comes a sharp sword with which to strike down the nations, and he will rule them with a rod of iron. He will tread the winepress of the fury of the wrath of God

the Almighty. On his robe and on his thigh he has a name written, King of kings and Lord of lords. (Revelation 19:11–16)

After reading these passages, you should fully realize that we do not live in a "safe" world. "Stay Safe" and "Be Safe" are wishful delusions in a world surrounded by cosmic violence. We opened this chapter with a scene torn from the pages of the classic C. S. Lewis novel *The Lion, the Witch, and the Wardrobe*. Mr. Beaver delivers two promises to young Susan: Aslan isn't safe, but Aslan is good.

In Lewis's story, Aslan (Lewis's Christ figure) is a lion and the rightful king of Narnia. In case you didn't know, lions are not safe, but certainly powerful, beautiful, and majestic. Not coincidently, Jesus is referred to as the Lion of the Tribe of Judah in Revelation 5:5. You can see from the Scriptures quoted in the previous paragraphs that God is a warrior who fights for you, and Jesus is one fierce God-man.

As we grow in our faith, we are called to become more Christlike day after day (2 Corinthians 3:18; Romans 12:2). Followers of Jesus should be kind, loving, and compassionate because that is Christlike. And likewise, followers of Jesus should also be strong, disciplined, fierce, and full of truth for the same reason. I personally find the right balance on occasion, but often, I find myself waffling between the two—brutish and harsh one day, then too soft the next. That's why we need Jesus.

Throughout the Bible, Jesus is given many names, including King of Kings, Prince of Peace, Lamb of God, Lion of Judah, and so on. We can't pick and choose our favorite attributes of Jesus and ignore the others. We can't say Jesus was 90 percent love and 10 percent judgment. Jesus is complete and perfect. He embodies 100 percent of all the righteous attributes. To be clear, Jesus is 100 percent Lamb of God and 100 percent Lion of Judah. That's what we are called to be.

The Space Between

Let's close this chapter with an illustration from world history. World War II was the most devastating and costly war of all time. The human loss was staggering: low estimates are fifteen million dead military personnel and thirty-eight million civilian deaths. The economic destruction is almost impossible to calculate. The European theater of the war officially ended with the surrender of Nazi Germany on May 7, 1945. However, most historians agree the war was effectively over by mid-June 1944. Allow me to explain.

On June 6, 1944, the Allied powers initiated Operation Overlord, better known as the D-day Invasion. It stands alone as the greatest amphibious attack in the history of warfare. On D-day, approximately six thousand ships and landing craft delivered approximately 160,000 Allied troops to storm the beaches of Normandy, France, to open a western front on the European continent. By midday on June 6, the bloodred beaches of Normandy were littered with bodies and wreckage. The German defense was stout, but through fierce determination and overwhelming numbers, the Allied troops secured the beachheads.

By June 12, 1944 (D-day plus six), the Allied forces advanced all the way to the French town of Carentan, which finally connected all the Allied bridgeheads in Normandy. The Allied invasion would not be turned back into the sea. The Germans were on the run. The Western Front was officially established as more men and material streamed onto the beaches of France. The Germans were effectively boxed in. American forces were applying pressure from the south (Northern Italy), the Russian hordes were advancing in the east, and the remaining Allies were now closing in from the west. Almost all tacticians at the time and historians today agree that the war in Europe was won. It was only a matter of time.

But someone forgot to tell the Germans.

They did not surrender until May 1945, eleven months after D-day. So, what happened in the space between June 6, 1944, and May 7, 1945? Pain, suffering, death, destruction, and carnage. There were almost a million total casualties in that time period. Everyone could see the eventual outcome of the war, but there would be a price to pay to get there. Christians, men of God, please hear me; we live in "the space between." I'm referring to the era between the resurrection of Jesus and His return. The resurrection of Jesus is the turning point of the human race. When Jesus uttered his last words, "It is finished," he defeated death and the scourge of sin. Simply put, it was game over for the Enemy. He won the ultimate victory over Satan and sin when He was resurrected from the dead. Because of this, as followers of Christ, we can walk and live in victory today.

His victory is our victory.

And if that weren't enough, Jesus is coming back. I've read the last book of the Bible. I know how it ends. As mentioned earlier, Jesus returns, leading an army of angels. He imprisons Satan, eventually killing him. The Scriptures say every knee will bow and tongue confess that Jesus is Lord

(Philippians 2:10–11). It's a terrifying yet spectacular ending. That time will come, but at a moment unknown to us. In the meantime, we live in "the space between." And much like our World War II illustration, although victory is secured, there will be much suffering before He returns. This is the reality in which we live. That's why we struggle and suffer from pain, loss, violence, hunger, and so on.

In World War II, the fighting didn't stop on June 6, 1944. Although victory was inevitable, there was much work to be done. Brothers, the pain and suffering didn't stop at the resurrection of Jesus. There is much work to be done. Dare I say, much fighting to be done.

I said once before: This world is full of problems. You were created to solve at least one. Where do you fit into God's big story? He has a plan for you. He molded and crafted you as a masterpiece (Ephesians 2:10) to be used as an implement of the master. God has a will, a desire, for each one of us. If we pursue His will for our lives, we will find joy, and He will be glorified. It's the reason for our existence.

He has never called us to be "safe." He has never desired us to be "comfortable." His desire is for His creation to seek the will of their Creator. His will is your purpose. We are called to seek His will and valiantly live out our God-given purpose. Let's kill, once and for all, the phrase "Safety first!" It's not even second. God's will is your purpose. Safety is a distant third priority. Because there is no safer place than the center of God's will.

CHAPTER 19

HIS WILL, YOUR PURPOSE

The Christian life is less about cautiously avoiding sin than about courageously and actively doing God's will.

—Eric Metaxas, *Bonhoeffer: Pastor, Martyr, Prophet, Spy*

God's will is your purpose, safety third. Let that sink in deep, become part of your very being. Despite the chaos of the day, I honestly believe I was safe on September 11, 2001. I know that sounds crazy, especially after reading my story. But it's true. I was surrounded by the pitfalls of death, yet I was safe. How can that be? Only because I was "courageously and actively doing God's will."

Read the opening quote by Eric Metaxas again. Metaxas has written, in my opinion, the definitive book on the life and death of German pastor Dietrich Bonhoeffer. The quote above is Metaxas's summation of Bonhoeffer's worldview in regard to Christian living. Many Christian men, myself included, focus their time and efforts on simply avoiding sin, being a "good guy," never causing a problem, just making it through without screwing something up.

The result is our lives resemble a man tip-toeing across a minefield, terrified of stepping on the next mine (sin). Picture that scene in your mind: a fearful man, head down, staring at his next footfall, focused on balance, never confident in his next step. At times, my life resembles this illustration. Men, answer me this: Would a wife or children feel secure following this man across the minefield?

To be clear, I'm not saying we should be reckless with sin. Sin is wrong and always brings greater consequences than we anticipate. I'm just proposing a different mindset regarding our primary focus. Our primary objective should be "courageously and actively doing God's will" in our lives. The natural byproduct of that obedience will be a life marked by joy and contentment in serving him, not sin. Now, let's return to our illustration. What if instead of focusing on the mines, the man locked in on the path God has already set before him? The minefield has already been mapped, and God has revealed your individual "safe" passage route through the field.

Imagine that scene for a moment: a confident man, head up, eyes locked on the horizon, boldly following a clear path, knowing he is safe and secure as he follows God's path (His will). Same question: Would a wife and children follow this man? Yes, without a doubt.

The Bible makes it clear that God has designed each of us for a purpose. We belong to Jesus (Romans 1:6) because we were created through Him and for Him (Colossians 1:16). And as the created, we were made to bring the Creator glory (Isaiah 43:7). Therefore, I want to keep working toward helping you discern and execute God's specific will for your life, enabling you to live with valiant purpose. To get there, let's begin with a wide aperture and then filter down to the individual. The Bible explicitly reveals God's will for all believers, narrows the scope further for Christian men, and then emblazons each believer's heart with a specific purpose or purposes. To ignore any level in God's plan is to actively disrupt His perfect order.

God's Universal Will for All Believers

Throughout the Scriptures, we find God explicitly stating the way in which all Christians should walk out their faith and execute His universal will. Remember: I'm just a guy, not some lofty theologian. Therefore, I certainly will not dissect each and every one in these pages. But some examples would include that He actually implores us, desires us, to seek His will (Ephesian 5:17). God specifically calls on all believers to abstain from sexual immorality (1 Thessalonians 4:3–4). God instructs all believers to help the weak, rejoice in all things, be content in all circumstances, and pray without ceasing (1 Thessalonians 5:16–18). We could go on and on, but let's revisit one of the primary objectives of God that serves as part of His universal will for all believers. It's commonly referred to as the Great Commission.

It is God's will that His followers make disciples and spread the word of His truth to all corners of the globe. In case you're wondering, that would be the far-off corner of the world consisting of unreached people and groups, as well as the neighbors living around the corner. Honestly, my personal track record here is mixed at best. Sometimes, I'm bold in sharing my faith, and other times, I shrink back like a coward. But I am encouraged by the promises of God in passages such as this. We already discussed this in chapter 7 but something this significant is worth repeating. Jesus spoke in Matthew 28: 18–19:

> All authority in heaven and on earth has been given to Me. Go, therefore, and make disciples of all the nations, baptizing them in the name of the Father and the Son and the Holy Spirit, teaching them to observe all that I have commanded you. And behold, I am with you always, to the end of the age.

Regardless of who you are and where you live, if you are a believer in Jesus, then you share in this great mission. To *go* and make disciples of all nations. Where Jesus is not known, there is darkness, and we are called to bring the light. And to be clear, that light is Jesus, the light of the world. This mission unites all Christians together in a shared purpose and it is, at some level, a part of your individual valiant purpose. Evangelism is the will of God. If your assignment sounds daunting, then focus on the final words of Jesus in Matthew's gospel: "And behold, I am with you always, to the end of the age."

There it is again. God is a "with-you" God. Jesus's final words in Matthew serve as a beautiful echo from a promise made in Isaiah 7:14 and reiterated in Matthew 1:23. The promise that the Messiah would be conceived from a virgin and he shall be called Emmanuel, which means "God with us." In the final scene of Matthew's gospel, Jesus reminds his followers, and us, that He will always be with us. For how long? Until the end of this age, upon His final return. We are not alone in our universal mission to spread the gospel to all nations.

Therefore, as Christians, it is our universally shared purpose to do one of two things. Point people to the light or be a representation of the light in this dark world. I charged earlier in chapter 7: "Be the man, standing in the alley, pointing people to Jesus." As believers, that is our common charge to keep. And make no mistake, when sharing the gospel, you are in the fight, committing an act of spiritual violence against the Enemy.

The apostle Paul wrote in 1 Timothy 2:3–4, "This is good and acceptable in the sight of God our Savior, who wants all people to be saved and to come to the knowledge of the truth." It's clear and obvious. God's desire is for all people to be saved by putting their faith in Jesus. His desire for your good and His glory. That is the calling. Will you answer the bell?

God's Design for Men

Now, let's begin to narrow down God's will and plan to the next level. God has prescribed a specific will, or purpose, for Christian men. Again, this is a deep subject matter on which entire books have been written. My plans for a second book include a deep dive into such topics. But for this space, I want to highlight just two fundamental, uniquely masculine callings from the Lord.

In the beginning, after God created everything from nothing, He created man. God gave man dominion over all His creation. He placed Adam in the Garden of Eden with two assignments. Genesis 2:15 states, "The Lord God took the man and put him in the Garden of Eden to work it and keep it." The man's first responsibilities before the woman was created were "to work and to keep" what God had entrusted to him.

We can break that into two simple commands. "To work" means to be a provider, which means cultivating the resources and relationships God has put into your care and placed under your responsibility. "To keep" means to protect the same. There it is, men. Let's keep it simple. It is God's will for all Christian men to be providers through work and cultivation and to protect all He has put under your dominion (1 Timothy 5:8). Let's tackle one at a time.

When a farmer works his land, it's more than plowing the field one time, planting the seed, and waiting for the harvest. He must cultivate the land. He turns over the good soil, waters it, prunes the growth, and so on. Cultivate means to promote or improve the growth of something through labor, attention, and training. Similarly, a man must cultivate what has been placed in his sphere of influence in order to provide for himself, his family, and his community.

We are called to cultivate the resources (occupation/career) given to us and the relationships (wife, family, friends) blessed upon us. Biblical provision is much more than working a forty-plus-hour week and coming home with a paycheck that covers the bills. It also means cultivating a career with time, wisdom, and effort that honors God and offers a brighter future for your family. We are to work hard with all our hearts, not to please man, but as if working for the Lord (Colossian 3:23). The end result is a financial provision that brings security and stability to your family and glory to God.

However, a man's calling to provide or cultivate is much more than material provision. In the book *Tender Warrior*, former Green Beret and pastor Stu Weber puts it this way:

"The physical necessities of life are the simplest, easiest duties of the provisionary. A little food, a little shelter, and physical provision is a done deal. But that isn't real provision. Thinking that food, clothing, and shelter equal provision is like confusing sex with love. Yes, it's a rather significant part of the story, but it isn't the whole book . . . We revert to the things we can see, when in fact it is the unseen world, the world of the spirit, the world of relationships, where we ought to be majoring in our provision. Matters of character, heart, spirit, integrity, justice, humility—the kinds of things that last. The character traits that outlive a man and leave, not a monument, but a legacy."[5]

In my opinion, Weber's *Tender Warrior* establishes the best prototype for the balanced provider and protector. As mentioned in chapter 18, Jesus is a warrior fighting on our behalf. In addition, Jesus serves as the perfect model of compassion, tenderness, and sacrifice. Simply put, Jesus is both 100 percent the Lamb of God and the Lion of Judah, all the time.

First, we must not conflate dominion with domination. A dominion mindset denotes a genuine care for others, those under your responsibility. The domination mindset is one of a selfish thirst for power. Simply put, we aim for service over self. Indeed, we are called to live upright lives and to cultivate relationships with the people placed in our care. I'm speaking of our families—more specifically, our wives and children.

So, what does it look like to cultivate in this realm? It means putting in the effort to improve their growth through labor, attention, and training. Cultivation of the family is a

---

5   Stu Weber, *Tender Warrior: Every Man's Purpose, Every Woman's Dream, Every Child's Hope* (Random House, 1995).

collaborative effort between husband and wife, with you leading the way. That includes leading in selflessness and sacrifice, leading in having hard conversations, and leading in modeling service and humility. It means modeling for them the "Lamb of God" aspects of Jesus in regard to patience, compassion, and grace. We are called to build up and pour into our wives, encouraging them to grow in their faith and God-given abilities. That starts by loving our wives unconditionally, like Christ loves His church (Ephesians 5:25), so that she will become like a fruitful vine (Psalm 128:3).

Men, we are called to bring our children up in a secure and healthy home. We are commanded to create an environment in which our children can grow bold in their faith and eventually become implements of God's love in this world. This requires you to train your sons and daughters. A father's calling is to raise them up in the disciplines and instruction of the Lord through the Word of God (Ephesians 6:4). Cultivation requires effort, patience, discipline, and care. It doesn't happen overnight, but your labor will bear fruit. This is an aspect of the will of God for all men.

A Man Protects What Has Been Entrusted to Him

Adam was also charged "to keep" or protect the garden. Therefore, men are called to protect all that God has entrusted to them. This includes the physical realm of his land, home, and especially his family. In addition, we are also charged to protect our families in a spiritual sense. In short, we must model the "Lion of Judah" for our families. First, let's tackle the physical world. Men, it's about to get real. Let's talk man to man, meaning bluntly. It is the will of God that you possess the capability and capacity to defend your property, family, and others who cannot defend themselves. And on occasion, that may require violence or the threat of violence. Contrary to what your mommy may have told you, sometimes violence is the answer. That's because evil doesn't stop when you ask nicely.

We are called to push back the darkness and fight evil as ambassadors for Christ. Evil in our present age must be confronted. Sometimes, that will require violence. Please hear what I am not saying. I'm not declaring it is the will of God for us to commit acts of random, rage-filled violence. But it is His will for you to be prepared to physically defend those placed in your care. Because sometimes, not often, evil will transcend the spiritual and confront you physically face to face. Therefore, when an intruder enters your home or your family is being robbed on the street, you will be required to stand toe to toe and go blow for blow to protect those placed in your care.

You are a guardian.

A godly man must possess both the capability and capacity to physically combat evil in the protection of his area of dominion. I'm about to get personal, so prepare for your sensibilities to be ruffled. The capability to protect your property and family involves being proficient at arms, physically fit, and possessing the ability to fight. Period. When seconds count, the police are only minutes away. You cannot assign this duty to others.

This is not an impossible task. You do not have to be some "mad dad" version of Jason Bourne. But, men, it is your responsibility to, at the very least, be capable. For example, make the time to learn the basics of properly deploying a handgun and ensuring its safe storage. If you don't know how, then pay for professional training to learn the basics. A firearm is not the only way to protect your dominion, but in my opinion, it is the best way. Make the time to become physically fit. You don't have to commit your life to CrossFit or competing in Ironmans, but this will require at least four hours a week to train your body for strength and endurance.

Fact: If you are overweight and weak, you will not have the ability to physically protect those in your care when it matters most.

That is not meant to shame anyone but rather to make you aware of the basic requirements. It is your responsibility to become physically fit. Additionally, make the time to learn some basics of hand-to-hand combat. Just start with some simple techniques (easily found for free online), and maybe you will find a passion for a particular discipline. Dip your toe into something: boxing, jiu-jitsu, martial arts, krav maga, and so on. But at a minimum, learn to throw a real punch and handle yourself on the ground.

I train my sons in the basics of striking and grappling and when to apply them. I teach them what my father taught me. You only fight to protect yourself or defend those in your care who can't protect themselves. I apply that standard to myself and, every day that I can, get a little better. You do not need to become an expert, just proficient. If this sounds like too much to handle, then tackle at least one of these issues and continue moving forward to the next.

In Nehemiah 4, the enemies of Israel are surrounding the Hebrews on all sides as they attempt to rebuild the wall around Jerusalem. Therefore, Nehemiah responded to the threat with ordinary men, not soldiers: "Then I stationed men in the lowest parts of the space behind the wall, the exposed places, and I stationed the people in families with their swords, spears, and bows . . . Do not be afraid of them; remember the Lord who is great and awesome, and fight for your brothers, your sons, your daughters, your wives, and your houses" (Nehemiah 4:13–14).

For whom are you willing to fight? In the battle of the "trained" versus the "untrained," the trained man almost always wins. Remember: when seconds count, the police are only minutes away. No one is coming to save you. You must become capable.

There are two sides to the coin of physical protection. You must also have the mental capacity to unleash righteous violence to protect those you love. You can train yourself as prescribed above, but ultimately, you must become comfortable with the decision to commit righteous violence in combating evil.

Both the Old Testament and New Testament offer scriptural support for righteous violence in combating evil (Proverbs 24:11; Psalm 94:16; Psalm 144:1; Luke 22:36–38). Make the decision now by becoming comfortable on the moral high ground found in the Bible. Run the scenarios through your head daily. How will I respond if (*fill in the blank*)? Only then will you react effectively in an emergency situation. I'm not saying to become paranoid about threats around you. I'm challenging you to be prepared for threats around you. Paranoia is fueled by fear. Preparedness is driven by wisdom and training.

I'm sure to have offended some in the preceding paragraphs. That's OK. We can respectfully disagree. But let's agree on the calling God has placed upon us, while maybe we disagree on the execution of that calling. For example, you may have a deep-seated moral belief against owning a gun (or maybe your wife does). Obviously, I feel differently, but I'm not likely to convince you otherwise on these pages. So, let's meet on the common ground that a man should arm/equip himself with something to serve as a force multiplier in a confrontation—whether it's a knife, baseball bat, five-iron, or anything in addition to your two hands to help you neutralize a threat.

One more note. If you're currently not physically fit, that's OK. But please begin the work toward better fitness. Not only will you slowly become a better protector, you will reap the plentiful physical and mental benefits of a healthy diet and exercise. The time is now. You can do this.

It is God's will for you, as a man, to protect all He has placed in your care. Get fit, get armed, get trained, and always be ready!

Spiritual Protection Is Required Every Day

The men of God must also provide spiritual protection for those placed in our dominion. Preparing for a physical confrontation is necessary, but thankfully, most of us will never be called upon in such a scenario. But I guarantee you will need to frequently stand in the gap to protect in the spiritual realm.

The best way to arm yourself spiritually is the consistent study of the Word of God because it is the sword of the Spirit. Even Jesus himself used Scripture to thwart the temptations (attacks) of the Enemy (Matthew 4). In addition, prayer is often the battlefield of the spiritual warrior. Some of the most powerful moments of my parenting life have been when my wife and I fervently prayed together for our sons. On a few occasions, we have felt the presence of the Enemy in our home. In those moments, we have stood shoulder to shoulder, demanding the Enemy to leave our home in the name of Jesus.

Make no mistake: These are acts of spiritual, or cosmic, violence in the heavenly realm referred to in Scripture. "For we do not wrestle against flesh and blood, but against the rulers, against the authorities, against the cosmic powers over this present darkness, against the spiritual forces of evil in the heavenly places" (Ephesians 6:12). Prepare yourself to spiritually defend those you love through prayer and arm yourself with the sword of the Spirit, which is the Word of God (Ephesians 6:17).

In the weeks following 9/11, President Bush began referring to himself as a "wartime president," and he was correct. We must grab hold of the same mindset in our homes. You are a "wartime husband" and a "wartime father."

Cultivation and provision often require a man to emulate Jesus, the Lamb of God. The role of protector calls on a man to model Jesus as well, this time as the Lion of Judah. As author Richard Phillips notes, "Our basic mandate as Christian men is to cultivate, build, grow (both things and people), but also to stand guard so that people and things are kept safe—so that the fruit of past cultivating and nurturing is preserved."[6]

Capability is forged from hard work and sweat. Mental capacity results from standing firm on moral grounds to

---

6   Richard D. Phillips, *The Masculine Mandate: God's Calling to Men* (Ligonier Ministries, 2016).

make the horrifying decision of when to commit righteous violence in defense of the weak. The godly man who rightly provides for and protects his family will offer a secure place for them to flourish.

G. K. Chesterton once wrote, "A real soldier does not fight because he has something that he hates in front of him. He fights because he has something that he loves behind his back."[7] Remember the battle cry of Nehemiah. Remember for whom you fight.

Allow me to put a personal spin on an old favorite, that quote attributed to George Orwell. Be the man whose family sleeps peacefully at night, knowing that a "rough man stands ready" to bring violence on their behalf. That's what it means to "quell the storm and ride the thunder."

7 G. K. Chesterton, *Collected Works of G. K. Chesterton: The Illustrated London News, 1905–1907* (Ignatius Press, 1986).

CHAPTER 20

WHAT IS MY MISSION?

Therefore I urge you brethren, by the mercies of God,
to present your bodies as a living and holy sacrifice,
acceptable to God, which is your spiritual service of
worship. And do not be conformed to this world, but
be transformed by the renewing of your mind, so that
you may prove what the will of God is, that which is
acceptable and perfect.

—Romans 12:1–2

In the years following the terrorist attack of 9/11, I struggled mightily with a lack of mission and meaning. On September 12, 2001, I got down on my knees to pray and begged the Lord to reveal His mission or calling on my life. I knew I should have died (twice!) the previous day, and the news was reporting that thousands of people had not been as fortunate as me.

Oddly, I never asked the Lord why I was spared and others perished. I felt I wasn't entitled to an answer to such a profound question. I just prayed. My simple prayer went something like this: "Lord, I am yours. I get it. I should have died yesterday, but for some reason, I didn't. Therefore, you must have a plan for my life. You now have my attention. Jesus, I am a good soldier. So, what is my mission? What are my marching orders? What do you want me to do with my spared life?"

Men, I said that prayer almost every day for five years and heard nothing in response. In that span of time, my marriage suffered, and I almost walked away from the Secret Service. I was a frustrated young Christian, and I took it out on the people closest to me. I was suffering from a disease. An ailment inflicted upon most men today, especially Christian men. I call the disease, *purpose lost*.

"Just Let Me Use You"

God began to forge me into an implement of His will long before I had a clue. In 2005, I finally "heard" a response from the Lord. After walking through my simple prayer, he graciously threw the four-hundred-pound gorilla off my back. He said to me, "Just let me use you." That's it. No clear path forward. No grand strategy. Just heed my call and obediently follow me. He illuminated my mind to the truth of this promise: "I created you perfectly to be used for good works, according to my will, in my perfect timing." It's as if he smacked me on the back of the head and said, "Just do the next thing." I didn't have all the answers, but I had clarity.

Not long after, Heather became pregnant with our first son. My immediate mission was crystalized: Raise this boy in the disciplines of the Lord, selflessly protect and love your wife, and cultivate an environment in which he matures into a godly man. Little did I know, God was just getting started. Several more sons followed, four in total, and God stoked a fire in my belly for Christian ministry to men.

Then He dropped the hammer.

As the ten-year anniversary of the 9/11 attacks approached, He made it very clear that it was His will for me to tell my story. I initially resisted because I was fearful. At that time, about a dozen people in the world knew the details of my 9/11 experience because it was just too painful to talk about. But the Lord blessed me with gentle nudgings to pursue His will. In due time, I was sharing my 9/11 experience with groups in an effort to share the gospel. My heart soared, and significant mental and emotional healing took place just from being obedient to His will. This book is a furtherance of my mission. It is part of the valiant purpose for which I was created. I'd like to help you discern yours.

Discernment of God's will and the courageous execution of His plan is the secret sauce to living a joy-filled life that brings glory to God. We'll tackle discernment in this chapter and execution in chapter 21. Teaching discernment of God's will is deep theological water on which entire books have been written. Now I was a rescue swimmer, but this is a different kind of water. In an effort to "keep it simple," I will draw from a biblical mind that has a knack for distilling complexities down into practical terms. Therefore, much of the content to follow in this section will be derived from the writings of modern theologian Jim Denison.

Denison brilliantly makes the deep water of theology seem like wading in the kiddie pool. I mean that as a compliment because many of us are simple-minded, like me. You can find much of Denison's work at thedenisonforum.org. Specifically, I will draw from an essay titled "How to Know God's Will," written in 1999, and another essay from 2018 titled "Right and Wrong Ways to Know God's Will."

The Four Keys to Discerning God's Will

Denison first establishes four foundational principles on which to build when discerning God's will. First, God indeed has a specific plan for your life, and it's a good plan (Jeremiah 29:11). Second, God deeply desires you to seek and know His will for your life. Third, the primary key to God's will is His Word. His plan will never call you to contradict His Word. Last, God's will is for you today, meaning now, not a five-year plan. Do the next thing now!

Understanding the will of God begins with giving your life to him. Let's examine the passage quoted to open the chapter, Romans 12:1–2. The apostle Paul is clear that God is the ultimate source of all things, through His power, and He is the very point that everything exists (Romans 11:36). Therefore, since this is true, we are to "present your bodies as a living sacrifice, acceptable to God" (Romans 12:1). Our "sacrifice" laid upon the altar is our very being.

To the Hebrews of that age, the "body" meant everything—mind, body, and soul. According to Denison, in a practical sense, that means our work, time, play, and material possessions, all of our lives given to Him.

Continuing, Romans 12:2 states we are to "not be conformed to this world." This simply means our outward acts and inward conditions should be completely different from the culture around us. A man cannot go with the flow of culture and simultaneously be a fountain of living water. To paraphrase Denison once again: our culture values stuff over people, popularity over principles, and present comfort over eternal life. No, we must be different. Paul continues by stating we are to "be transformed by the renewing of your mind"

(Romans 12:2). Transformed would encompass an outward change in actions that match the inward metamorphosis of our redeemed nature, which is a Spirit-filled heart.

Furthermore, the "renewing of your mind" only happens as the Holy Spirit corrects our thinking through consistent prayer and study of the Bible. Denson wraps up his analysis succinctly: "If you have transferred ownership of your life to God, withdrawn from the world's account, and are investing daily in your relationship with Jesus, you are in the will of God. Then you will be able to test and approve what God's will is—his good, pleasing, and perfect will. And then you will find and fulfill your life calling and ministry."[8] The result is a natural following of God's will in obedience to His plan, not necessarily a knowledge of His plan.

This mirrors my experience following 9/11. I prayed for God to give me the "marching orders" of His will, but He simply wanted me to be obedient to His Word and His calling, one small step at a time. Let's hear from Denison again: "He may reveal his will through Scripture, circumstances, other people, or by speaking to you intuitively (the Holy Spirit). But if you are willing to go anywhere and do anything, when you need to know his will, you will. The question is not one of knowledge, but obedience."[9]

You may be thinking, *Self, all that sounds hard.* Yes, because it requires us to lay down our selfish desires and be obedient to His desires. I have wasted years of my adult life ignoring God's calling on my life. Sometimes, I ignored it, and

8   Jim Denison, "How to Know God's Will" (Denison Forum: October 17, 1999).

9   Jim Denison, "Right and Wrong Ways to Know God's Will" (Denison Forum, June 24, 2018).

other times, I was downright defiant. But through His grace, I have been given this opportunity to share my message with you. I am now living out my valiant purpose because He is faithful and patient. Remember: there is no safer and more fulfilling place to be than the center of God's will. The key to walking boldly and effectively for Jesus, the (un)Safe Life, is to live out your God-ordained purpose.

Here are some other benefits to living this (un)Safe Life. When executing God's purpose for your life, your works will bear good fruit. You will increase in your knowledge of God, be strengthened by the power of His might, and experience a heart full of joy and thanksgiving. How does that sound? Pretty good, right? In Colossians 1:9–11, Paul informs the recipients of his letter that he prays for them without ceasing that

> you may be filled with the knowledge of His will in all spiritual wisdom and understanding, so that you will walk in a manner worthy of the Lord, to please him in all respects, bearing fruit in every good work and increasing in the knowledge of God; strengthened with all power, according to His glorious might, for attaining of all steadfastness and patience; joyously giving thanks to the Father.

There it is, hiding in plain sight. What does a divine-purpose-driven life look like? Pleasing to God, fruitful, powerful, steady, patient, and joyfully grateful. Would you want to be described in such a way? I would. Pastor and theologian John MacArthur says, "Spiritual wisdom and understanding is not only the knowledge of biblical principles but also the application of those principles to daily living." We can only "increase in the knowledge of God" through the Spirit-led study of God's Word and intimate prayer with our Creator.

In conclusion, God's will is always revealed through the Holy Spirit and His Word. And the two will never contradict each other. His Spirit is alive and dwells in the heart of every believer (1 Corinthians 3:16), and it will "guide you into all truth" (John 16:13) as you walk with Jesus.

The Spirit not only counsels but also provides previously unattainable power and strength to the believer. His Word is the reference point from which everything makes sense. His Word is mighty and powerful. His Word is perfect, inspired by God, and useful for teaching, correction, and training in righteousness so that "the man of God may be adequate, equipped for every good work" (2 Timothy 3:16–17). God's Word will equip you to walk in a manner worthy of the Lord.

The study of His Word reminds us of who God is and what He can do through the power of His might. What can He do through you? By yourself, you do not have what it takes, nor do I. But by His Word and through His Spirit, He is a "with-you" God that created you for a purpose. Take heart. It sounds difficult; it's not. It sounds risky; it's not. It sounds fulfilling; it is.

Jim Denison's conclusion is spot on. Denison writes, "God has a plan for Adam and Eve—where and what to live. A plan for Noah—how to build his ark, right down to the exact specifications and building materials he should use. A plan for Abraham, including where he should live, how old he would be when he had his son, and even that son's name. A plan for Joseph, using his slavery and imprisonment to save the entire nation. A plan for Moses, encompassing the very words he should say to Pharaoh. A plan for Joshua, showing him where and how to take the land. A plan for David and Solomon, for their kingdom and the temple they would build for him. A plan for Daniel, even in the lion's den. Jesus had plans for his first disciples—plans they could not have begun to understand. He had a plan for Saul of Tarsus as he left to persecute the Christians in Damascus. He had a plan for John on Patmos. Now God has a plan for your life."[10]

Your valiant purpose is part of His big story.

Pastor, Rebel, Spy

Let's briefly examine the life of a godly man with a valiant purpose. It's time to revisit our good friend from chapter 19, Dietrich Bonhoeffer. Bonhoeffer was not a physically impos- ing man. He was an academic to the core. He was a pacifist through much of his adult life. By our modern cultural stan- dards, Bonhoeffer was not physically impressive. But he was a spiritual titan. Bonhoeffer's life was one marked by fiercely following God's will regardless of the circumstances. As you will see, God's will was his safe harbor.

Bonhoeffer was a Christian pastor in Germany during the rise of the Nazi Party. The greater German church was largely silent as Hitler rose to power, brutally crushing all opposi- tion. Bonhoeffer was one of the few loud voices speaking out against the evils of Nazi ideology. Over time, he became a target of Hitler and his Gestapo thugs.

10   Jim Denison, "Right and Wrong Ways to Know God's Will" (Denison Forum, June 24, 2018).

Europe was on the brink of war when many of Bonhoeffer's friends and colleagues pleaded with him to flee the country before it was too late. Bonhoeffer resisted their cries for a time but eventually gave in to their wishes. He bowed to the will of man, not the will of God. So, he fled Germany, crossed the Atlantic by ship, and arrived in New York City in June of 1939. He had previously been offered a position to teach and preach at a church in the Bronx. Bonhoeffer was far from the reach of Hitler, far from the threat of arrest, and far from the ravages of the looming war. Bonhoeffer was safe, at least by the world's standards. In reality, there was war raging in his soul. Bonhoeffer knew, deep in his guts, that he was not supposed to be in New York. He could not escape the calling of his mighty God. Only two weeks later—yes, just two weeks—he returned to Nazi Germany. He willingly entered into the lion's den because he knew it was the will of God for his life, his very own valiant purpose.

Upon arriving in Germany, he picked up where he left off. Bonhoeffer began to travel from village to village, preaching boldly against the evils of the Nazi Party. He created a "seminary on the run" as he taught the truth of the gospel in defiance of the Nazis. Eventually, Bonhoeffer secretly worked for the German Resistance, serving as a courier for resistance members within the German intelligence community. He even made contact with members of British intelligence and may have been involved in an assassination plot targeting Hitler himself. It's amazing how courageous a man of God can be when he knows he is being obedient to the will of his loving God. The opposite of fear is love.

However, the Gestapo (Nazi Secret Police) eventually caught up to Bonhoeffer and arrested him in April 1943. Dietrich Bonhoeffer was executed by hanging in a German prison in April 1945 as the Nazi regime collapsed under the Allied assault. Author Eberhard Bethge offers a stunning quote from his book *Dietrich Bonhoeffer: A Biography*. Bethge quotes a Nazi doctor who witnessed Bonhoeffer's execution:

> I saw Pastor Bonhoeffer . . . kneeling on the floor praying fervently to God. I was most deeply moved by the way this lovable man prayed, so devout and so certain that God heard his prayer. At the place of execution, he again said a short prayer and then climbed the few steps to the gallows, brave and composed. His death ensued after a few seconds. In the almost fifty years that I worked as a doctor, I have hardly ever seen a man die so entirely submissive to the will of God.[11]

Dietrich Bonhoeffer answered the call God had put on his life. He had transferred ownership of every aspect of his life to Christ. His inward renewal was outwardly evident as he swam against the stream in opposition to the Nazi majority. His fierce commitment to God's will was steady and strong to the end. As he approached the gallows, he was "brave and composed," with a strength and steadfastness only found in the Lord. And his "work" was fruitful for generations.

God created Bonhoeffer for that moment. He was made for the Nazi era in Germany to fulfill God's purpose, for God's glory.

---

11   Eberhard Bethge, *Dietrich Bonhoeffer: A Biography* (Fortress Press, Revised Edition 2000).

He returned from the "safety" of America to fulfill the purpose for which he had been created. He actively and courageously confronted evil with truth. The love of Christ drove him deeper into danger while simultaneously overcoming his fear. Ultimately, he died "entirely submissive to the will of God." In April 1945, Dietrich Bonhoeffer was stripped naked and executed by hanging in a German prison yard. However, I would argue he wasn't naked at all. Because he died in a dirty suit.

CHAPTER 21
FIGHT THE GOOD FIGHT

Blessed be the Lord, my rock
Who trains my hands for war,
And my fingers for battle;
My faithfulness and my fortress,
My stronghold and my deliverer,
My shield and He in whom I take refuge.
—Psalm 144:1–2

Men, it's time to execute. In the last few chapters, we have discussed one aspect of God's universal will for all Christians, that being to spread the good news of Jesus Christ while making disciples in all the nations. We also examined the common purpose shared by all Christian men, to work and to keep all that God has placed in our care. In the last chapter, we dug into ways in which we can discern God's will or purpose for our personal lives. Following discernment, comes the effort to carry out God's purpose for your life.

Think of the last few chapters as a holy football huddle. God, the quarterback, gives the play (His will), and now it's time to break the huddle and execute the play. Please forgive the clunky metaphor, but go along with me here. Men, no one celebrates a great huddle! Glory is not found on the practice field. Glory is not won in the team film room. Practice and film study are necessary for success, but glory is won on the field of play. God's glory is won when we courageously follow His will and execute his purpose for our lives as a part of his big story. But it's no game. This is real life. And it's no ball field. It will often resemble a battlefield. But this is where the "good stuff" of life is found.

Here, we find joy, contentment, and fulfillment. This is where God gets the glory, and we receive the humble honor of being used as an implement of His holy righteousness. This is where we bring the light into the darkness. This is where we make good trouble for the Enemy. But be aware. If you execute your God-given valiant purpose, then that makes you dangerous to the Enemy. Ha! There's no safer place to be.

Check out our opening passage for this chapter, Psalm 144:1–2. Read it again. It's a reminder of who God is and the reality the Bible is not always a rated-PG story. I wish I could say I came across that verse in a Bible study, but that would be a lie. I first heard this passage from the lips of Parker as he sniped German soldiers in a scene from the classic 1998 movie *Saving Private Ryan*. Thank you, Tom Hanks and Steven Spielberg.

In the scene, Corporal Parker is placed in a bell tower, running sniper overwatch. One by one, he places the crosshairs on the enemy and pulls the trigger while reciting this verse. What a cool scene. But I had never heard or read this passage before, probably for two reasons. One, in 1998, my personal time in the Bible was grossly lacking. And second, you will rarely (if ever) hear such a verse uttered today from a pulpit in the American church. That's a fact.

But Psalm 144 is clear. We need a fortress, a stronghold, a deliverer, and a shield. Why? Because we are living in a spiritual battle, and the minute you begin to execute your God-given purpose, you step onto the battlefield. The Enemy's first move is to take you out of the fight before you enter the fray. You may have been taken out of the fight with porn and lust. Or you bought the lie that career success would bring ultimate happiness, so your efforts were purely material. Or maybe you were just perpetually distracted with shiny, fun things like fantasy football and binging on Netflix. Regardless, you were rendered combat ineffective.

But not now, not today. Once you pursue God's will and actively live out your purpose, you become a threat. But fear not. The Lord, through your steadfast obedience, has "trained your hands for war and your fingers for battle." Time to make some good trouble.

Worth Fighting For

The apostle Paul refers to this battle as "fighting the good fight of faith." He uses this phrase three times in Scripture, all in his letters to his young disciple Timothy. Paul gives Timothy a charge to keep when he instructs, "This command I entrust to you, Timothy, my son, in accordance with the prophecies previously made concerning you, that by them you fight the good fight, keeping faith and a good conscience" (1 Timothy 1:18–19).

Men of the Christian faith, we, too, are called to defend the gospel of Jesus Christ. Paul continues in chapter 6 of the same letter:

But flee from these things, you man of God, and pursue righteousness, godliness, faith, love, perseverance and gentleness. Fight the good fight of faith; take hold of the eternal life to which you were called. (1 Timothy 6:11–12).

Men, there is your charge to keep. Take firm hold of the life to which you have been called and fight the good fight! In so doing, pursue the good stuff of life, like righteousness (found only in Christ), faith, gentleness, and perseverance. Pastor John MacArthur writes of this passage: "The man of God is known by what he flees from, follows after, fights for, and is faithful to."[12] I challenge you to lay that description over your life and see how you measure up. If you're like me, you probably fall woefully short. But you can move forward with the full confidence of your right standing with God through Jesus. We are not called to be perfect, but we are called to become more Christlike, one degree at a time.

"Fight the good fight of faith," Paul commands. According to MacArthur, the Greek word for *fight* used in that passage provides us with the English word *agonize*. *Agonize* denotes a fierce struggle with intense effort and was used at that time regarding athletics and military endeavors.[13] It's clear this fight will not be easy, and it will not be pretty. But trust me: you were built for this.

In Paul's final instructions to his mentee, he once again references the good fight of faith. Paul, while rotting in a

12   John MacArthur, 1 Timothy 6:11, *The MacArthur Study Bible* (Thomas Nelson, 2006).

13   MacArthur, 1 Timothy 6:12, *The MacArthur Study Bible*.

Roman prison and fast approaching martyrdom, writes this as he completes his second letter to Timothy. "For I am already being poured out as a drink offering, and the time of my departure has come. I have fought the good fight, I have finished the race, I have kept the faith" (2 Timothy 4:6–7). May the same be said for all the men of God Who valiantly pursue and execute the will of our Father.

Take heart, men. "Do not fear, for I am with you; Do not anxiously look about you, for I am your God. I will strengthen you, surely I will help you, surely I will uphold you with my right hand." (Isaiah 41:10). Conflict didn't end with the Old Testament. Trouble didn't cease with the resurrection of Jesus. Remember, we live in the space between the resurrection of Christ and his second coming. Therefore, there is physical conflict in this world that is spawned from the spiritual battle happening all around us.

To be clear, the Scriptures are quite specific. Our enemy is not our fellow man but rather "against the cosmic powers over this present darkness" (Ephesians 6:12). We fight the schemes of the Enemy, not flesh and bone. The physical conflict in our present age, caused by sin, results in pain and suffering. This physical conflict is the byproduct of the ever-present spiritual war. Look around. Everywhere, there is brokenness: wars, starvation, disease, drug addiction, child sex trafficking, cheating, fatherless families, the killing of unborn babies. Unfortunately, I could go on and on. This world is full of problems, but I believe you were created to help solve at least one.

God has created you uniquely with certain strengths and abilities. You have been created one of a kind, for good works, to be carried out by you and only you (Ephesians 2:10). That being said, recite the words of David as you cry out, "Make me to know your ways, O Lord; teach me your paths. Lead me in your truth and teach me, for you are the God of my salvation; for you I will wait all the day long"(Psalm 25:4–5). Consider this as your personal prayer; "Lord, I'm an obedient warrior who wants to make good trouble for the Enemy. Where do you want me in the fight?" Have you ever posed such a question to the Lord? We all share roles in the universal aspects of God's will. But He created us each differently, even perfectly, for a specific mission set. Men, there is an arena waiting for its gladiator. In that arena, you will find pain, brokenness, suffering, and abuse. This is why God created good, strong men. Fight the good fight. You are being called to enter the fray, answer the bell, do the next thing. Your arena awaits.

Welcome to the Thunderdome

Speaking of an arena, let's hear from our old friend Teddy Roosevelt. Previously, in chapter 9, we drew some lessons on being a true citizen from Roosevelt's well-known address "Citizenship in a Republic." Now, let's finish with the most famous excerpt from Roosevelt's speech regarding "the man in the arena" and how we can apply it to our Christian walk.

It is not the critic who counts; not the man who points out how the strong man stumbles, or where the doer of deeds could have done them better. The credit belongs to the man who is actually in the arena, whose face is marred by dust and sweat and blood; who strives valiantly; who errs, who comes short again and again, because there is no effort without error and short-coming; but who does actually strive to do the deeds; who knows the great enthusiasms, the great devotions; who spends himself in a worthy cause; who at the best knows in the end the triumph of high achievement, and who at the worst, if he fails, at least fails while daring greatly, so that his place shall never be with those cold and timid souls who neither know victory nor defeat. Shame on the man of cultivated taste who permits refinement to develop into fastidiousness that unfits him for doing the rough work of a workaday world.[14]

Men, it's time we all get our faces "marred by dust and sweat and blood." It's time to "strive valiantly" in executing God's purpose for your life. It's time to be the one who "spends himself in a worthy cause." Be the man in the arena!

When we picture the arena in our minds, many probably think of Maximus the Gladiator. Some may imagine the football gridiron with twenty-two men smashing into each other. A few, like me, may envision the boxing ring or a UFC octagon. But real life isn't movies and ballgames. Real life has real consequences: honor, pain, glory, suffering, victory, defeat. Even life and death.

We Need More Heroes

What is your arena? By that, I mean, where have you been called into battle? You have been fashioned and purposed by your Creator to be an implement of spiritual violence in the

14 Theodore Roosevelt, "Citizenship in a Republic," speech given at the Sorbonne in Paris, France, April 23, 1910.

heavenly realm. Look around you. Wherever you see broken-ness, the Enemy has a stronghold. Which stronghold have you been designed to bust wide open? That is your arena.

Take time to intentionally pray and examine the world around you, especially where you have influence. Find the pain, the suffering, the problems, the dark spaces of soci-ety. Now ask yourself and ask the Lord, *What grieves my soul? What issue/problem provokes me to righteous anger or breaks my heart, longing to bring compassion? What issue/problem moves me to tears?* Just ask, and the Holy Spirit, who lives within you, will reveal it. It could be any issue: homelessness, teenage pregnancy, fatherless homes, foster care/adoption, drug addiction, mentorship, domestic violence.

Identify one and then get after it.

Spend the rest of your days getting your suit dirty in an effort to bring the love of Christ into the problem. No doubt some of you are thinking, *Forget societal problems. My own house is burning!* OK, I get it. If you are not currently culti-vating and protecting all God has placed in your dominion, then that is your arena. In fact, there is no more important place to get your suit dirty.

Others of you may be considering a career change because you feel called elsewhere. Yes, if you are being obedient to the will of God, then go for it. That's your next arena. In all of these spaces, as with Roosevelt's man in the arena, you will make errors, and you will fail at times. But you will at least fail "while daring greatly," and you will never be one of those "cold and timid souls who neither know victory nor defeat." Again, I ask, what is your arena?

One of my "arenas" is the issue of child sex trafficking. All over the world, and especially in the United States, children are used as sex slaves by adult boys who masquerade as men. To say the issue provokes righteous anger in me is a gross understatement. But that's only the tip of the iceberg. Child sex trafficking hurts me to my very core. I feel it in my guts. The Holy Spirit has made it clear to me that I am built for this fight. Over the last few years, I have had the privilege of donating some of my free time to an antitrafficking ministry in the Dallas-Fort Worth area. Now, in my post-USSS career, I plan to get significantly more involved in this fight. In many ways, my Secret Service training and experiences have prepared me for this challenge. I believe God provided me with such a career for this very fight and others.

In my church alone, I have witnessed God bringing together a variety of people with very different skills and abilities to attack this scourge in our area. On one occasion, I was part of a four-person team in a car conducting community outreach for the child sex trafficking ministry. Our team of four (two men and two women) prayed aloud in the car as we drove to our target area. One of these women is a complete spiritual prayer warrior. She also is living out her calling. She prayed powerfully for God's safety and provision and, ultimately, that we would locate some of the missing young girls in our area.

As she wrapped up the prayer, she paused for additional words from her teammates. At that point, I closed the prayer with "Lord, equip and enable us to go punch the Enemy in the throat."

Everyone chuckled as we said amen, except for our prayer warrior female. She looked at me with resolve in her eyes and said, "That's exactly what we're gonna do." Now that's a team. We, through the power of the Holy Spirit, were balanced in our approach. Loving and fierce. Compassionate and battle-ready. The Lion and the Lamb.

Men, I implore you to find your arena in which to battle the evils of this world because it is part of God's valiant purpose for your life. You will find no greater joy and fulfillment than to do the will of God, to fight the good fight. Everyone is different and uniquely wired by God. What moves my soul to action may not even elevate your heart rate and vice versa.

But do not fight alone in the good fight. Find your like-minded people. Remember my 9/11 experience. I was *always* more effective when I was with "my guys." We fight better shoulder to shoulder, shield to shield! The Enemy wants you to be alone and distracted. He does not want you to be purpose-driven and united with fellow brothers and sisters in Christ. Let your love for Christ and your hatred of sin drive you in your endeavors.

Remember: we follow a "with-you" God Who equips us with everything we need for the journey. Being the man in the arena fighting the good fight is literally bringing the light of Jesus into the dark spaces. It will not be pretty or without failure. It will not be easy, and it will not seem "safe." But it will be good. Because there's no safer place to be than the center of God's will.

Be Like Max

In the 2000 film *Gladiator*, there's an intense scene in which the hero, Maximus, is forced to identify himself to the evil emperor. Maximus, blood on his hands from combat in the arena, removes his battle mask to reveal his true identity. He stares defiantly into the eyes of the shaken emperor and declares, "My name is Maximus Decimus Meridius, Commander of the Armies of the North, General of the Felix Legions, loyal servant to the true emperor, Marcus Aurelius. Father to a murdered son, husband to a murdered wife, and I will have my vengeance, in this life or the next."

Whoa! If you've seen the movie, then you appreciate the scene and its raw power. I desire something similar for each of you. To fight the good fight in the arena for which God has created you. To win, to lose. To strike and to be struck. To dare greatly and wreak good trouble in the name of Jesus. I pray I will have the courage to do it myself.

Imagine yourself in that *Gladiator* scene. I'll speak from the first person, but in your mind, place yourself there:

Sweat pours from my body, and blood drips into my eye. I wipe my brow and steady my feet for another attack.

The Enemy shakes his head in disbelief and asks, "Who are you?"

I answer with strength and courage born only from the Lord: "My name is Darin Kinder, loyal servant of the one true God, a faithful husband, a devoted father, and a fierce adopted son of the King. God's will is my purpose. Prepare to be punched in the throat."

EPILOGUE

Well, this has been an incredible journey. Thank you for believing in this message and for your heartfelt desire to boldly live out your God-ordained purpose. Those in your sphere of influence will reap the benefits, and God will receive His fitting glory and honor.

I pray you learned some valuable lessons as told through the lens of my experience in the World Trade Center on September 11, 2001. May we never forget the nearly three thousand citizens we lost on that tragic day.

If this book can bring any amount of good into the world from that tragedy, then I have accomplished one of my goals. My primary objective for this project is to help unleash the men of God on the world in a way that brings the love of Christ to those who need it most. I've talked much about fighting and spiritual warfare, but it is all driven by love. Compassion is God's love in action.

I have written this book specifically with men in mind. That's because I believe part of my personal valiant purpose is to minister to men. Therefore, I have obediently devoted much of my life to fulfilling this calling. Christian women were not the target audience of this book, but they certainly share a vital role in this endeavor. Women are equally valuable in this fight, and they, too, are created for a purpose that brings God glory. They have different skills and abilities that must be brought to bear in this fight as well. They are a blessing to the man of God, as he is a blessing to her.

Men, here is your call to action. Your arena awaits. Be the man pointing others to Christ as you bring the light of Jesus into this present darkness. Jesus won the ultimate victory, and you are His ambassador. Remember: the opposite of fear is love. Let the love of Christ overwhelm your fears as you pursue your valiant purpose in life because courage is a choice. Get your suit dirty—daily. A dirty suit is the result of investing daily in the good work of your occupation and the intentional cultivation of the relationships in your sphere of influence.

Your charge to keep is also the protection, both physical and spiritual, of those cherished ones placed in your care. Believe me, the man of God who actively "works and keeps" all that has been entrusted to him does so in a dirty suit. The Christian walk is fully embraced when one willfully submits to God's will and then actively and courageously executes it. Altogether, I call that "Fighting the Good Fight." His purpose for you will lead to an arena in which you make an impact for the Kingdom of God, the arena where I can think of no greater place to get your suit dirty.

Bury Me in a Dirty Suit is also the launching point for my new men's ministry initiative, titled Fierce Faith. If you have enjoyed the content and tone of this book, then you will love what we are doing at Fierce Faith. We are reclaiming intense biblical manhood, one household at a time. Visit *fierce-faith.com* and *darinkinder.com* for more information. But it starts with you. I'm calling you to a path chosen by only a few rough men who quell the storm and ride the thunder by valiantly seeking and pursuing Jesus and the purpose He has emblazoned on their hearts.

Jesus said, "Enter by the narrow gate. For the gate is wide and the way is easy that leads to destruction, and those who enter by it are many. For the gate is narrow and the way is hard that leads to life, and those who find it a few" (Matthew 7:13–14). In this passage, Jesus was speaking of ultimate salvation and in whom or what we place our faith. This passage makes three promises I would like to highlight. One, following Jesus leads to true life. Two, following Jesus will be hard. Three, very few will make that choice.

I think we can also apply this lesson to our walk as men, courageously living out God's will. Most men in our current age will not choose the narrow path. They will take the "easy" path that leads to destruction. But the men of Fierce Faith will take the narrow path. The hard way. I call it the "dirt road." When I punch out of this world and into the next, bury me in a dirty suit. I pray the same for you.

Now may the God of peace, who brought up from the dead the great Shepherd of the sheep through the blood of the eternal covenant, that is, Jesus our Lord, equip you in every good thing to do His will, working in us that which is pleasing in His sight, through Jesus Christ, to whom be the glory forever and ever, Amen.

—Hebrews 13:20–21

ACKNOWLEDGMENTS

Thank you to the brave men and women of the first responder community. You are underpaid and underappreciated, but we would be lost without you. Keep going! The valiant men and women of the United States Secret Service answer the bell every day. It was an honor to serve with you for twenty-five years. Moving forward, the mission is only getting more difficult. Press on. It was the honor of a lifetime to stand shoulder to shoulder on 9/11 with the rough men and women of the USSS New York Field Office. John Buckley, Tom Armas, Rob Donovan, John Beck, and Frank Larkin were the best of the best on 9/11. Thank you for leading by example and giving this young man the courage to fight the good fight.

Good friends matter. Their faithful devotion encourages a man when he succeeds and picks him up when he stumbles. I've had some of the best. Jack, Joel, and Ted, I love you for life. Brian F, Chris Y, Rich, Will, Chris E, and Brian G are my band of brothers and a gift from God. Thank you. My father was a good man but not a spiritual mentor. But the Lord timely placed godly men in my life to serve as spiritual mentors: Lee McGraw, ED Clem, Houston Shirk, Tommy Nance, Hal Habecker, and Rankin Gassaway. These men have been spiritual titans in my life. Thank you for modeling biblical masculinity to me.

Special thanks to Blake Atwood and Tom Dean for teaching me so much about the writing/publishing industry. This project would never have launched without you. Eddie Jones, my thanks to you for your guidance and suggestions during the writing process. Adam Tarnow has never given me a bad piece of advice. I can never repay you for your insights and friendship.

The team at Streamline Books has been nothing short of exceptional. Will and Alex, you have created an incredible place that enables regular people like me to share their stories with the world. Thank you. Donnel McLohon, you have been my good shepherd through this process, and I am grateful. It's not easy to copyedit a manuscript from a first-time author, but Ginny Glass was up to the task. Mandi Reed, your fingerprints are all over the best parts of this book. Thank you for your tireless editing efforts and firm guidance. You went above and beyond because you believed in the project. I am grateful.

My father didn't live to see this book come to fruition. He was a good father and I know he would have been proud of me. He gave me a fierce fighting spirit. Mom, you are the best. Your love and support over the years have shaped the man I have become. Thank you for modeling true faith to me at a young age. Doug, as my brother, I can say you have always been the real cop in the family. You are a model of hard work, loyalty, and integrity. I couldn't ask for a better big brother.

Sam, Nate, Ben, and Daniel: each of you is a cherished gift from the Lord. I am humbled to be your father and so proud of the men that you are becoming. You have seen me at my best and worst, yet you still love me unconditionally.

You are literally part of my valiant purpose in life. Thank you for believing in me and keeping me grounded. I can't imagine life without you.

Heather, you are the reason I fight to live a godly life. You inspire me to be a better man. Your faith in Jesus has encouraged me in my own walk with the Lord. You are the perfect partner, not to mention the best boy mom in the world and definitely the toughest member of our family. I love living life with you. Let's keep going!

ABOUT THE AUTHOR

DARIN KINDER is a former Special Agent of the United States Secret Service, where he spent decades protecting world leaders and navigating high-stakes environments. On September 11, 2001, he was on the ground in New York City when the World Trade Center was attacked, an experience that earned him the Secret Service Medal of Valor and forever shaped his faith and perspective on life.

Beyond his career in federal service, Darin is a devoted husband and father to four sons and founder of Fierce Faith Ministries. He is passionate about inspiring and equipping the next generation with unwavering faith and teaching them to pursue their God-given purpose with courage. A sought-after speaker and podcast guest, Darin shares his insights on leadership, resilience, and the bold call to live a life of valiant purpose.